ATLAS OF
GEOLOGY AND
LANDFORMS

Written by
CALLY OLDERSHAW

FRANKLIN WATTS

A Division of Scholastic Inc.
New York • Toronto • London • Auckland • Sydney
Mexico City • New Delhi • Hong Kong
Danbury, Connecticut

Picture Credits t = top, b = bottom, c = center, l = left, r = right, FC = Front Cover

Ann Ronan Picture Library: 14tl, 24tl, 79c, 83tr. Chris Fairclough/ISI: 36tl, 84tl. Colorific: 21br. Corbis: 29cr, 47cr & 89cb, 58tl, 62cl, 74tl, 78/79b, 85t, 89r. FLPA: 39cr, 40cl, 40br, 41tr, 41bl, 42bl, 43tr, 45cr, 50tl, 56tl, 62c, 64cb, 82tl, 82/83t, 83br, 88br, 88/89t. Gamma: 24/25c, 25tr, 25bl, 30tl, 30cl, 31cr, 33cl, 60/61b. Geoscience Picture Library: 32tl, 44/45cb, 78bl. Image Select International: 17bl, 24bl, 29tr, 34cl, 34/35b, 36tl, 46tl, 46bl, 46/47cb, 50/51cb, 82b, 85br. J Allen Cash: 38cb, 66/67c. Library of Congress; 52/53b. Nasa: 9bl. Natural History Museum: 87tr, 87b. NHPA: 20/21t, 42cr, 42/43t, 76/77b, 77cr. Oxford Scientific Films: 31tl, 38/39ct, 49t. Pictor: 10cl, 28/29t, 30/31cb, 38/39b, 40tl, 41tl, 43cr, 46/47ct, 48/49b, 52/53t, 56/57cb, 59bl, 63bl, 65t, 65cr, 65bl, 72cl, 72/73t, 73cr, 76/77t, 80/81b, 84r, 85cl, 86cl, 86/87t, 87cr, 88cl. Science Photo Library: FCt. Ticktock Publishing: 68tl.

Produced in association with **ticktock** *Publishing Ltd.*

Writer: *Cally Oldershaw*
Co-writer: *Neil Morris*
Artwork: *Peter Bull Art Studio*
Picture research: *Image Select International*
Editors: *Felicity Trotman, Joyce Bentley*
Managing Editor: *Penny Worms*
Designers: *Graham Rich, Elaine Wilkinson*

Library of Congress Cataloging-in-Publication Data

Oldershaw, Cally.
    Atlas of geology and landforms / written by Cally Oldershaw.
      p. cm.— (Watts reference)
    Includes bibliographical references and index.
    ISBN 0-531-11774-X
    1. Geology—Juvenile literature. 2. Earth—Juvenile literature. [1. Physical geography. 2. Earth. 3. Geology.] I. Title. II. Series.

    QE29 .O63 2001
    550—dc21

                            2001027637

FOREWORD

If you were to travel back to 1750 and tell people that Earth is more than four-and-a-half billion years old; that mountains form when continents crash together; and that giant reptile-like creatures once roamed Earth, they wouldn't be very impressed. In fact, they would almost certainly ignore you, make fun of you, and possibly even lock you away.

In 1750, many people thought Earth was about 6,000 years old (5,754 years, to be exact). They thought that Noah's Flood had shaped the entire landscape and laid down all of the rocks, and that nothing had changed much since. Why did people believe this? They just looked at things in a different way.

In the late 18th century, natural philosophers (people we would call scientists) began to look at Earth in a new way. They examined rock formations and analyzed minerals. They watched rain fall, rivers flow, and volcanoes erupt. They measured gravity, magnetism, and the heights of mountains. They even experimented with making rocks in laboratories. All the while, they were thinking, trying to reason out the workings of Earth. Without consulting any books, they were slowly able to figure out why there are mountains, what causes earthquakes, and when Earth formed. Geologists recognized that Earth must be much older, and must have a much more interesting history than they had ever imagined.

When geologists look at sandstone, they don't see motionless and unchanging chunks of rock. They see the rock as it began millions of years ago, as the loose shifting sand of an ancient beach. A bed of coal in Antarctica evokes a warm tropical swamp, and a U-shaped valley echoes the creak and scrape of glaciers bulldozing the mountains. Rocks and landforms are the only reliable record we have of Earth's past; to a geologist, rocks are Earth's history books.

The fascinating information presented in this book comes from more than 250 years of observing, experimenting, and thinking by thousands of scientists. The colorful photos and illustrations will help you see the world through the eyes of these scientists and help you to understand how our planet was formed. If we're fortunate, we will continue to add to the information in this book, consulting Earth— and other planets—for centuries to come.

—Margaret W. Carruthers

Margaret W. Carruthers lives in Oxford, England. She has a M.S. in Geology from the University of Massachusetts in Amherst and a B.S. in Natural Resources from the University of the South.

CONTENTS

EARTH IN OUR UNIVERSE

The Universe is everything that we know. It contains billions of galaxies, collections of stars, and planets. Our planet is in a galaxy called the Milky Way and we orbit a star called the Sun. This section tells us how Earth fits into the solar system.

INSIDE EARTH

Activity within Earth creates movement on the surface, altering the structure of our planet. In this section, discover why volcanoes occur, where mountains come from, and why rocks are so important to geologists.

ON THE SURFACE

The atmosphere surrounding Earth produces weather cycles. These shape the landscape and give us climates. Lakes, islands, and vast oceans are all surface features that are in a continual state of change.

NATURAL RESOURCES

Humans are a recent arrival on Earth. In a short time we have learned how to extract rocks, minerals and fuel from Earth. We use these in every aspect of our lives. See how this affects our planet.

AN INTRODUCTION TO GEOLOGY

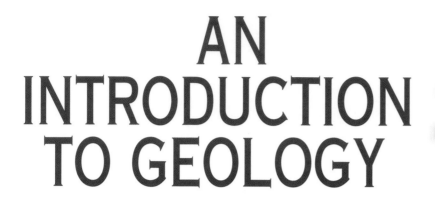

Geology is the study of planet Earth. Scientists who study Earth are called geologists, Earth scientists, or geoscientists. They study the history of Earth and the Solar System to try and understand how Earth formed, how old it is, and how it has changed over its lifetime. Geologists look at the rocks beneath our feet in order to understand how rock is made and how landscapes change over time. This helps them understand how our world looked in the past and how it will look in the future.

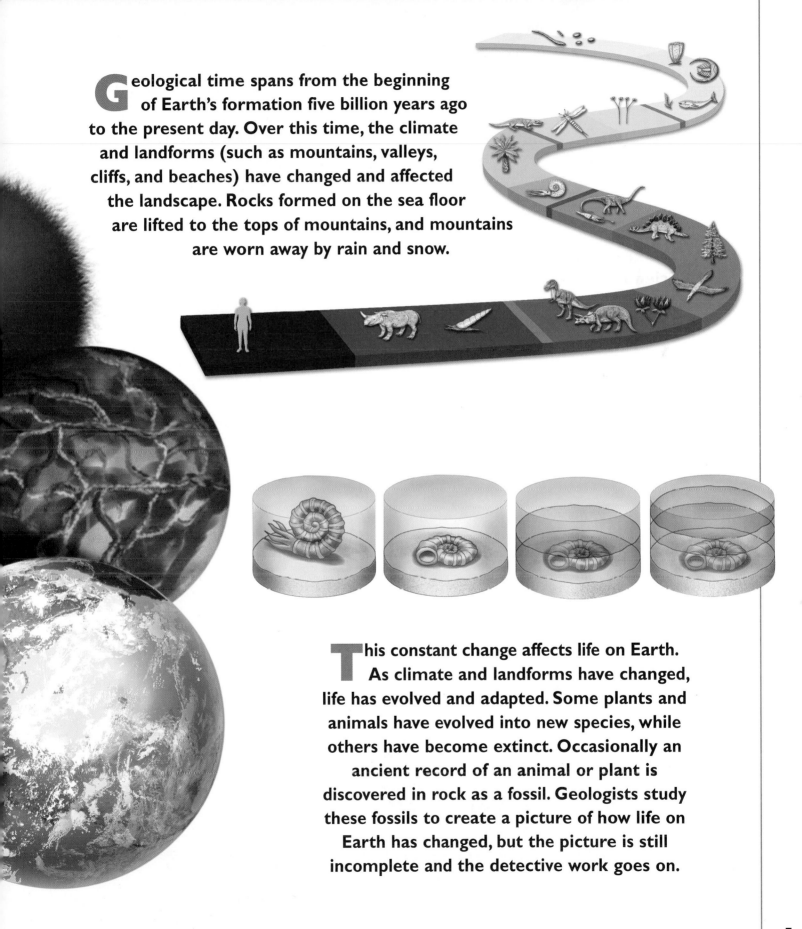

Geological time spans from the beginning of Earth's formation five billion years ago to the present day. Over this time, the climate and landforms (such as mountains, valleys, cliffs, and beaches) have changed and affected the landscape. Rocks formed on the sea floor are lifted to the tops of mountains, and mountains are worn away by rain and snow.

This constant change affects life on Earth. As climate and landforms have changed, life has evolved and adapted. Some plants and animals have evolved into new species, while others have become extinct. Occasionally an ancient record of an animal or plant is discovered in rock as a fossil. Geologists study these fossils to create a picture of how life on Earth has changed, but the picture is still incomplete and the detective work goes on.

EARTH AND THE SOLAR SYSTEM

DISTANCE FROM THE SUN

Planet	Million Km	Million Miles
Mercury	58	36
Venus	108	67
Earth	150	93
Mars	228	142
Jupiter	778	486
Saturn	1,427	891
Uranus	2,871	1,794
Neptune	4,497	2,810
Pluto	5,914	3,696

Earth is one of nine planets that travel around a star that we call the Sun. The Sun and its planets make up the solar system, along with moons and other objects, such as comets and pieces of rock called **asteroids**. Everything in this system, including our planet **Earth**, is connected to the Sun by the invisible force called gravity. The Sun is just one of billions of stars that cluster together in our galaxy—the Milky Way—and there are probably as many as one hundred thousand million galaxies in the Universe. All life on Earth depends on the Sun's energy, and so far as we know, Earth is the only place in the Universe where life exists.

EARTH'S ORBIT

As Earth travels around the Sun, it spins on its own axis, turning different parts to the Sun and giving us day and night. But Earth's axis has a slight tilt, so that north and south are not straight up and down as the planet orbits the Sun. This creates our seasons. When the northern half of the globe is tilted towards the Sun, it is summer there. At that time it is winter in the southern hemisphere, because it is tilted away from the Sun's warmth.

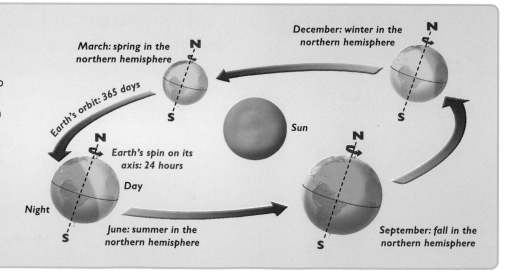

March: spring in the northern hemisphere

December: winter in the northern hemisphere

Earth's orbit: 365 days

Earth's spin on its axis: 24 hours

Day

Night

Sun

June: summer in the northern hemisphere

September: fall in the northern hemisphere

SUN

THE PLANETS

Earth is the third planet from the Sun. It takes just over 365 days (a year) for Earth to orbit the Sun. The closest planet, Mercury, takes just 88 days. The furthest planet, Pluto, takes 248 of our years to complete its orbit. All the planets spin on their axes and have day and night, just like Earth, but they spin at different speeds. Venus takes 243 of our days to spin round once, while Jupiter takes less than ten hours.

1. **Mercury** Mercury is a rocky planet, not much larger than our Moon. Like the next planet, Venus, it has no moons.

2. **Venus** Venus has a very thick atmosphere of carbon dioxide gas, which traps the Sun's heat and makes the planet very hot.

3. **Earth** Earth has a satellite, called the Moon, which travels around the Earth as it orbits the Sun. The Moon has a diameter just over a quarter as big as Earth.

4. **Mars** Mars is our nearest planetary neighbor. It is sometimes called the red planet, because its rocks and soil are colored by iron oxide.

5. **Jupiter** Jupiter is the largest planet in the solar system. It is a gas giant, made mainly of hydrogen around a rock-iron core.

6. **Saturn** Saturn is famous for its rings. It has seven main rings and thousands of smaller rings, made mainly of tiny pieces of rock coated with ice. Saturn also has 23 moons.

7. **Uranus** Uranus has 11 rings and 18 moons. Its rings are almost vertical because the planet has turned onto its side.

8. **Neptune** Neptune has eight moons, four rings and a Great Dark Spot, which is caused by a storm on its surface.

9. **Pluto** Pluto is the smallest planet and the farthest from the Sun. Some scientists think it is more like an asteroid than a planet.

◀ THE BLUE PLANET

Viewed from space, our planet looks mainly blue because most of its surface is covered by oceans. The white, swirling patterns are made by clouds, and outlines of the continents can also be seen from space. People were not sure exactly what Earth looked like from a distance before the first spacecraft took off in the last century.

EARTH'S FORMATION

Most scientists believe that the Universe came into existence about 15 billion years ago with a huge explosion, which we call the **Big Bang**. The explosion created the material of the Universe and caused it to expand, which it is still doing. Millions of years after the Big Bang, a thin cloud of expanding gas clustered into galaxies, which then formed smaller clouds that became stars. Our Sun formed in this way about five billion years ago. As the star became smaller and hotter, gas, dust, and debris collected together to form the planets, including Earth. The planets were also very hot, and Earth formed as a red-hot, molten ball.

METEORITES

The young Earth was constantly bombarded with **meteorites**—pieces of rock that came hurtling from space. Some of these rocks may have broken away from other planets in the solar system. As they crashed onto the thin skin of the forming Earth, the meteorites made deep, round craters. Meteor Crater, in Arizona (above), was formed in this way, but much more recently. This crater is 1,275 meters (4,180 feet) wide and 175 meters (570 feet) deep.

6. This is Earth as we know it today, but it will go on changing in the future. Activity inside the planet will produce changes that will reshape the continents and oceans.

1. The Sun formed as a spinning cloud of gas pulled together by gravity. Thick clouds of material around the star came together to form the planets and the rest of the solar system.

2. As Earth took shape as a red-hot, molten ball, heavier materials sank toward the center to form a **core**. Lighter materials came to the surface, and a thick layer of poisonous gases surrounded the sphere to form an early kind of **atmosphere**.

3. Over millions of years, the red-hot molten planet cooled enough for a **crust** to start forming. This early crust was made up of many blocks of cooling rock called komatiite. It floated on a sea of molten rock that was bombarded by showers of meteorites.

4. After the meteorite showers, things quieted down enough for Earth to cool, and the crust to thicken. Gases from volcanoes changed the atmosphere enough for rain to fall. Rainwater settled in depressions and **craters** in the oceanic crust, and filled the first oceans.

5. By 4 billion years ago, the crust was solid enough to form the first continents. These were surrounded by oceans. Beneath the oceans was oceanic crust that was made of basalt rock.

THERMOSPHERE TO EXOSPHERE
AND ON TO OUTER SPACE

80 km

MESOSPHERE

50 km

ozone layer

STRATOSPHERE

10-18 km

TROPOSPHERE

EARTH TODAY

Earth is made up of layers—both beneath its surface and above it. The planet itself is made up of four separate layers, including the thin outer shell of the crust. People once thought that Earth was completely solid, but the study of **earthquake** vibrations and other scientific methods revealed a different picture. Above the surface, Earth is wrapped in a blanket of gases that we call the **atmosphere**. Scientists also divide this into layers according to temperature. The air of the atmosphere, which gets thinner with increasing distance from Earth, is made up mainly of nitrogen and oxygen, with small amounts of other gases.

ATMOSPHERE

The first layer of the atmosphere above the planet's surface is called the troposphere, and it contains more than three-quarters of the mass of all the atmosphere's gas. The troposphere is warmest at ground level and coolest at its upper boundary, called the tropopause, the height of which varies above the equator and the poles. The second layer is the stratosphere, which contains the **ozone layer**—a band of gas that absorbs the Sun's harmful rays. Above the stratosphere are the mesosphere and the thermosphere. The very outer layer of the atmosphere, called the exosphere, begins at a height of about 700 km (430 miles) above Earth, and then the atmosphere gradually fades into outer space.

EARTH'S MAGNETOSPHERE

The magnetosphere is a region of strong magnetic forces surrounding Earth and stretching out beyond the atmosphere—up to 60,000 km from the planet's surface. The magnetosphere stops particles of solar wind—a continuous flow of electrically charged particles from the Sun—from reaching Earth's surface. Some of the charged particles are trapped by the Van Allen radiation belts surrounding Earth, and the solar wind squeezes the magnetosphere as it streams towards Earth, pushing it out of shape.

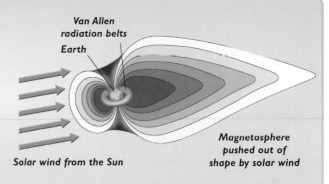

Van Allen radiation belts

Earth

Solar wind from the Sun

Magnetosphere pushed out of shape by solar wind

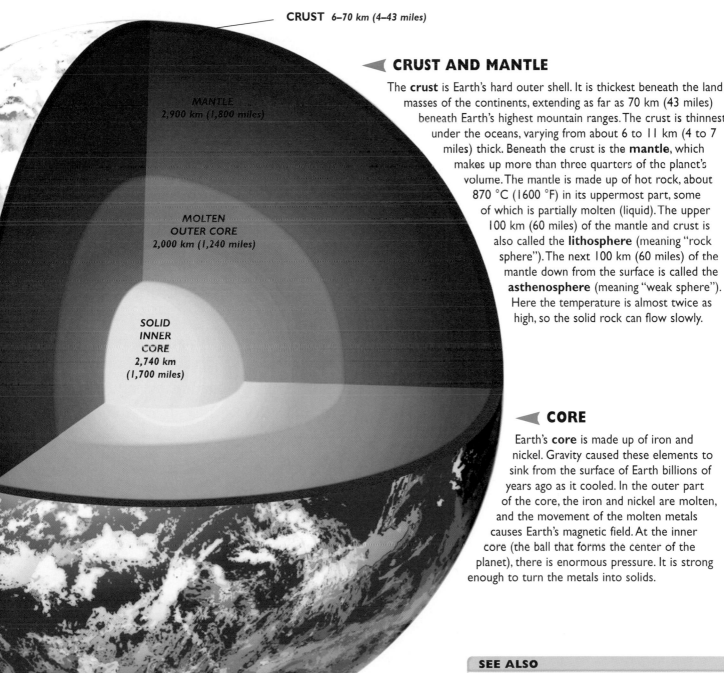

CRUST *6–70 km (4–43 miles)*

MANTLE
2,900 km (1,800 miles)

MOLTEN OUTER CORE
2,000 km (1,240 miles)

SOLID INNER CORE
2,740 km (1,700 miles)

◀ CRUST AND MANTLE

The **crust** is Earth's hard outer shell. It is thickest beneath the land masses of the continents, extending as far as 70 km (43 miles) beneath Earth's highest mountain ranges. The crust is thinnest under the oceans, varying from about 6 to 11 km (4 to 7 miles) thick. Beneath the crust is the **mantle**, which makes up more than three quarters of the planet's volume. The mantle is made up of hot rock, about 870 °C (1600 °F) in its uppermost part, some of which is partially molten (liquid). The upper 100 km (60 miles) of the mantle and crust is also called the **lithosphere** (meaning "rock sphere"). The next 100 km (60 miles) of the mantle down from the surface is called the **asthenosphere** (meaning "weak sphere"). Here the temperature is almost twice as high, so the solid rock can flow slowly.

◀ CORE

Earth's **core** is made up of iron and nickel. Gravity caused these elements to sink from the surface of Earth billions of years ago as it cooled. In the outer part of the core, the iron and nickel are molten, and the movement of the molten metals causes Earth's magnetic field. At the inner core (the ball that forms the center of the planet), there is enormous pressure. It is strong enough to turn the metals into solids.

SEE ALSO

| Earth and the Solar System | **pages 8–9** |
| Earth's Formation | **pages 10–11** |

LIFE ON EARTH

THEORY OF EVOLUTION

Most scientists believe that different forms of life on Earth developed and changed very slowly over millions of years. This gradual process is called **evolution**. In 1859 the British naturalist Charles Darwin (1809–82) published his theory of evolution in a book called *The Origin of Species*. It was based on findings he made during a five-year voyage around the world in a ship called the *Beagle*. Darwin believed that as conditions on Earth changed, they suited some animals better than others. Those animals which adapted easily to their surroundings survived, while those which did not, died out over time. Like Darwin, scientists today see the changes brought about by evolution by studying the fossilized remains of prehistoric animals and plants.

When our planet was still young, the steam from **volcanoes** turned into water in the cloudy **atmosphere** and fell back to Earth as rain. A vast ocean began to form, and it was here that life began, in the form of very simple organisms made up of just a single cell. Plant-like bacteria called blue-green algae probably first appeared more than three billion years ago in places where hot water bubbled up from cracks in the ocean floor. As light and heat from the Sun began to break up some of the ocean's water, oxygen was released into the atmosphere. When the first land plants appeared, more than four hundred million years ago, they created more oxygen. Conditions were finally right—after more than four billion years of Earth's history—for life on land. The regions of land, sea, and air that support life are known as Earth's **biosphere**.

Tertiary (65–2 m.y.a.) Birds and mammals flourish; primates evolve, and the first hominids about 6 to 4 m.y.a..

Quaternary (2 m.y.a.– present) Many mammals die out during ice ages; emergence of modern humans.

QUATERNARY

TERTIARY

GEOLOGICAL TIMELINE

Fossil finds in different layers of rocks have allowed scientists to build up a picture of how and when life on Earth developed. They divide the planet's history into various periods of time, beginning with the Precambrian era, which lasted from the formation of the planet to about 570 million years ago (m.y.a.). This era covers almost 88 percent of Earth's history! Over the following 500 million years life developed dramatically, but the first humanlike creatures—which we call hominids—only appeared some time between six and four million years ago. Scientists believe that modern humans evolved in Africa and began their migration to other parts of the world about one hundred thousand years ago.

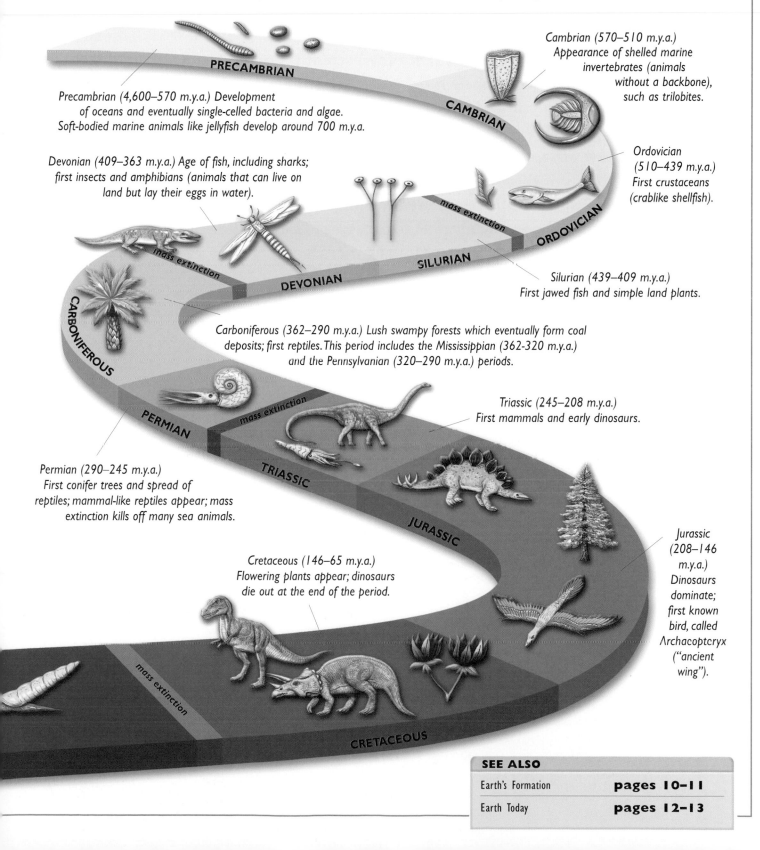

Precambrian (4,600–570 m.y.a.) Development of oceans and eventually single-celled bacteria and algae. Soft-bodied marine animals like jellyfish develop around 700 m.y.a.

Cambrian (570–510 m.y.a.) Appearance of shelled marine invertebrates (animals without a backbone), such as trilobites.

Ordovician (510–439 m.y.a.) First crustaceans (crablike shellfish).

Devonian (409–363 m.y.a.) Age of fish, including sharks; first insects and amphibians (animals that can live on land but lay their eggs in water).

Silurian (439–409 m.y.a.) First jawed fish and simple land plants.

Carboniferous (362–290 m.y.a.) Lush swampy forests which eventually form coal deposits; first reptiles. This period includes the Mississippian (362-320 m.y.a.) and the Pennsylvanian (320–290 m.y.a.) periods.

Permian (290–245 m.y.a.) First conifer trees and spread of reptiles; mammal-like reptiles appear; mass extinction kills off many sea animals.

Triassic (245–208 m.y.a.) First mammals and early dinosaurs.

Jurassic (208–146 m.y.a.) Dinosaurs dominate; first known bird, called Archaeopteryx ("ancient wing").

Cretaceous (146–65 m.y.a.) Flowering plants appear; dinosaurs die out at the end of the period.

PRECAMBRIAN

CAMBRIAN

ORDOVICIAN

SILURIAN

DEVONIAN

mass extinction

mass extinction

CARBONIFEROUS

PERMIAN

mass extinction

TRIASSIC

JURASSIC

CRETACEOUS

mass extinction

MOVING CONTINENTS

If you look at a present-day map of the world, you will see that the shape of the Atlantic coastline of South America looks as if it would fit neatly into the coastline of West Africa. This is no coincidence. Like all the continents of the world, these two land masses were once joined together. When scientists made the amazing discovery that the continents are constantly moving by tiny amounts, they realized that this had to do with the structure of Earth's outer shell. The **crust** is not made of one smooth surface, like an eggshell, but is cracked into huge pieces that fit together like a giant jigsaw puzzle. These pieces are called **plates**, and Earth's continents are the visible parts of these plates with the oceans covering the rest. The plates move slowly over the hot **mantle** beneath them. This means that the Atlantic Ocean, for example, widens by up to 5 centimeters (2 inches) each year, pushing South America and Africa, as well as North America and Europe, farther apart.

CONTINENTAL DRIFT

THE WORLD 200 MILLION YEARS AGO

Scientists believe that separate land masses drifted together to form one huge supercontinent about 250 million years ago. Plate movements meant that this supercontinent, which we call Pangaea, was ready to split apart again around 200 m.y.a. (see left). At that time Pangaea was surrounded by an enormous ocean known as Panthalassa (meaning "all sea"), which was the ancestor of the Pacific Ocean. The split would create Laurasia in the north and Gondwanaland in the south.

140 MILLION YEARS AGO

Around 140 m.y.a., Gondwanaland began to split apart, leaving a continent near the South Pole which included what was to become Australia. The land that was to become India split off and moved towards Asia. At the same time, the beginnings of the South Atlantic Ocean began pushing South America and Africa apart.

40 MILLION YEARS AGO

Australia split away from Antarctica, and India crashed into Asia, pushing up the crust to form the beginnings of the Himalayan mountain range. The Tethys Sea was closing up to become the Mediterranean, while the Atlantic Ocean continued to grow and force former Laurasia apart.

Scientists believe that this trend will continue in future and change the look of the continents. Some think that the Atlantic Ocean may start to shrink again in about 100 million years. The land masses may come together to form another supercontinent 250 million years from now.

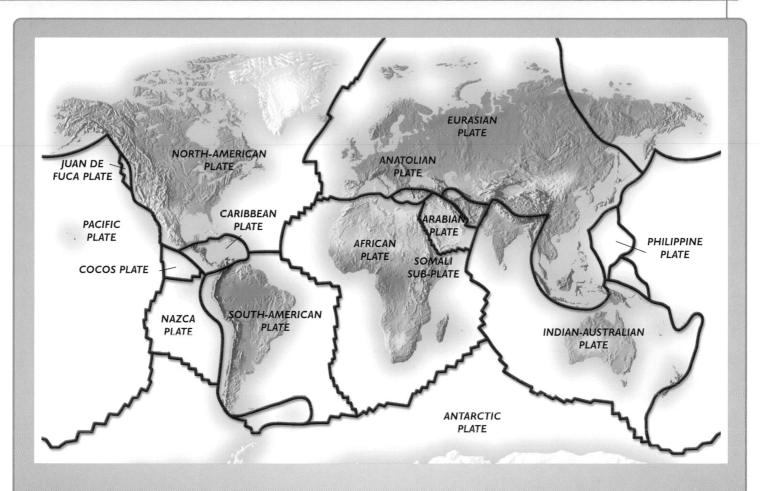

EARTH'S PLATES TODAY

Today, Earth's crust is split into fifteen major plates and many smaller ones. Some are continental plates, such as the Eurasian plate that carries the combined continents of Europe and Asia. Others, such as the vast Pacific plate, are called oceanic plates. The edges of plates form high ridges or deep trenches, which is where new crust is created and destroyed. Stable areas of plates, far from their edges, are called cratons. The oldest rocks on Earth are found in these areas.

◄ DISCOVERING THE JIGSAW

The theory of **plate tectonics**—the idea that Earth's crust is made up of moving rigid plates—developed from the first ideas about continental drift. These were presented in 1912 by a German meteorologist named Alfred Wegener (1880–1930) *(left)*, who had made many observations of the movement of land masses. Twelve years later his main work was translated into English as *The Origin of Continents and Oceans*. Other scientists disagreed with his ideas for many years, but by the 1960s, his theories had been proven to be correct and were generally accepted.

SEE ALSO

Earth's Changing Surface	**pages 18–19**
Effects of Plate Movement	**pages 20–21**

EARTH'S CHANGING SURFACE

The **plates** that make up Earth's **crust** are constantly moving, though very slowly and by only a few centimeters each year. This process and the huge forces involved create new landforms and destroy old ones over millions of years. Earth's plates move as a result of enormous forces called **convection currents** within the planet's **mantle**. These currents constantly force hot, molten rock—called **magma**—upwards toward the surface. In places where the magma reaches the surface itself, new crust is created and plates move apart. At the same time, long mountain ranges are created on the world's ocean beds. In other places, solid, cool crust is forced back down into the mantle, where it heats up and causes more magma to form. This also contributes to the creation of many of the world's **volcanoes** and **earthquakes**. The entire process of plate movement involves a never-ending cycle which constantly reshapes Earth's surface.

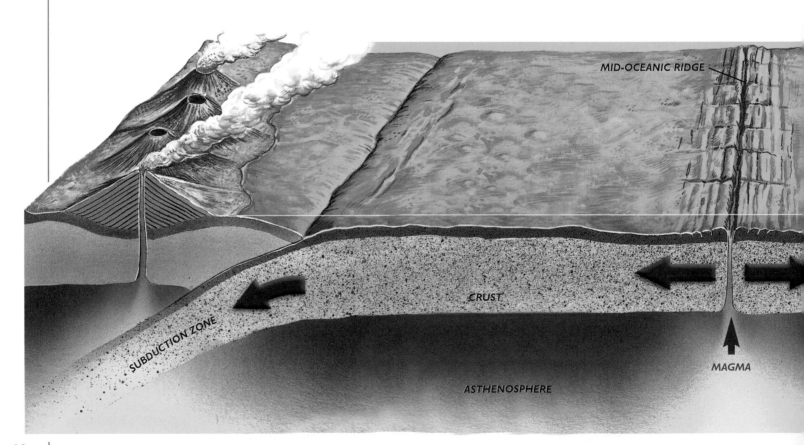

MID-OCEANIC RIDGE

CRUST

SUBDUCTION ZONE

MAGMA

ASTHENOSPHERE

CREATING AND DESTROYING CRUST

Earth's plates are constantly pushing together, pulling apart or sliding past each other. As they do so, it affects Earth's surface, either by creating new crust (at constructive margins), by forcing crust to be destroyed (at destructive margins), or by a simple shift of two plates (at conservative margins).

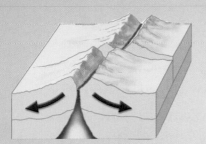 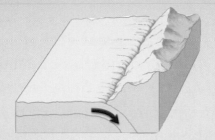 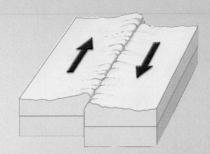

CONSTRUCTIVE MARGIN

When two plates pull apart, magma rises up from the asthenosphere, the upper part of Earth's mantle. As the magma cools, it becomes solid and forms new crust, which then moves slowly away from the ridge that forms between the two plates. This kind of plate boundary is called a constructive margin.

DESTRUCTIVE MARGIN

When two plates collide and push together, one of the plates is forced beneath the other in a process called **subduction.** *As one plate slips down into the asthenosphere, its rocks melt and become part of the mantle again. This kind of plate boundary is called a destructive margin, and the areas where they occur are called* **subduction zones.**

CONSERVATIVE MARGIN

When two plates slide past each other in opposite directions, they do not create new crust or destroy old crust. This kind of plate boundary is called a conservative margin. As the plates rub against each other, the grinding movement often causes earthquakes.

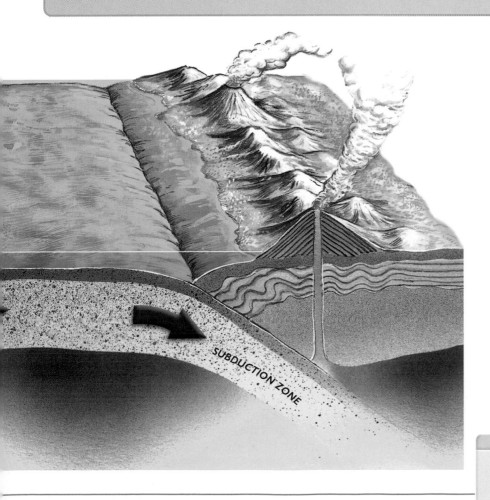

SUBDUCTION ZONE

◄ SPREADING RIDGE

On the ocean floor, constructive margins (*see above*) form **spreading ridges.** As magma from the **asthenosphere** reaches the surface and cools, it pushes up the ocean floor to either side of the plate boundary. This forms a ridge up to 1,500 meters (4,900 feet) high, creating a mountain range beneath the sea. The mid-ocean ridge may stretch along the sea bed for thousands of kilometers.

EFFECTS OF PLATE MOVEMENT

INDIA (as it is today)

Its position 50 million years ago

Its position 70 million years ago

There is great deal of activity along and near the boundaries of Earth's **tectonic plates** because of the huge forces involved. Although a great deal of the activity takes place beneath the world's oceans, it has a great effect on the continents too. As new crust is created at the Mid-Atlantic Ridge, for example, the ocean floor spreads and North America and Europe continue to move farther apart. Where plates are forced together and collide, the crust buckles and trembles. In some places high mountain ranges are pushed up, while in others **volcanic eruptions** remind us of how powerful these small movements are. The same is true of **earthquakes**, and the world's most destructive examples usually occur near **plate margins**. Other changes in Earth's surface are too small and happen too slowly to observe in a single lifetime, but over millions of years they alter the appearance of the planet.

▲ RAISING THE HIMALAYAS

India was originally an island in the Indian Ocean. The Himalayas were formed as India plowed northward into Asia. They uplifted Earth to create a mountain range reaching to heights of over 8,000 meters (26,000 ft). **Weathering** and **erosion** smooth the tops of the mountains, but the Himalayas are still rising upward as India continues to push into Asia.

MID-ATLANTIC RIDGE ▶

This **spreading ridge** runs all the way down the Atlantic Ocean, from north of Iceland to Bouvet Island in the south. The ridge stretches for about 11,300 kilometers (7,000 miles)—farther than the longest mountain range on land. Most of the ridge is deep beneath the surface of the ocean, but Iceland and Ascension Island are exposed parts. The Mid-Atlantic Ridge is on a constructive margin *(see diagram)*, where new crust is formed and slowly widens the Atlantic Ocean.

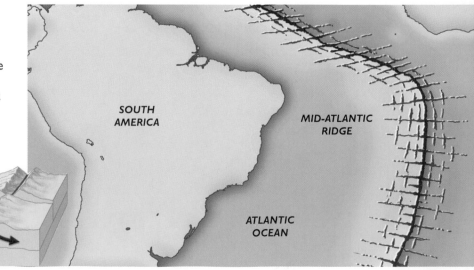

SOUTH AMERICA

MID-ATLANTIC RIDGE

ATLANTIC OCEAN

◄ VOLCANOES

The **volcanoes** of Indonesia have formed as a result of the Indian-Australian Plate **subducting** under the Eurasian Plate. Many volcanoes occur near **subduction zones**, often where an oceanic plate is forced beneath a neighboring continental plate at a destructive margin (see *diagram*). The forces and movement involved cause cracks in the continental plate and allow **magma** to force its way through an opening in the ground. This is how many volcanic eruptions occur.

AFRICA

SAN ANDREAS FAULT ►

The San Andreas Fault, along the coast of California, is a conservative margin (see *diagram*). The fault marks the boundary between the Pacific and the North American plates, which are moving past each other at a rate of 5 centimeters (2 inches) per year. It is 1,200 kilometers (750 miles) long and is one of the world's most active earthquake zones.

BODY WAVES

P WAVE

S WAVE

Primary waves (P waves) and secondary waves (S waves) are called body waves, because they travel through the body of Earth. P waves are like train cars colliding into one another. S waves move like a snake, from side to side through rock. The P waves travel at almost twice the speed of the S waves. P waves can travel through solid rock, deeper molten rock, water, or air. They are the first waves to be detected by scientists. S waves are slower and cannot travel through liquids.

EARTHQUAKES

An **earthquake** is a sudden, violent movement of Earth's **crust**. Earth quakes, which means that the ground shakes or shudders. The energy released travels as **seismic waves**, like ripples of water. Earthquakes occur all over the world, but the pattern is not random. Like **volcanoes**, most large earthquakes occur at the margins of **tectonic plates**, where one plate passes another or where two plates collide causing movement along faults within rocks. Nowhere on Earth is completely safe from them. Even if you have never felt the slightest seismic tremor, you will be aware of the devastation caused by earthquakes. At their mildest, earthquakes can be mistaken for the passing of a train or the effects of a gust of wind. At their most severe, they destroy roads, buildings, bridges and can even move hillsides. Architects and engineers face special problems in countries where earthquakes occur regularly.

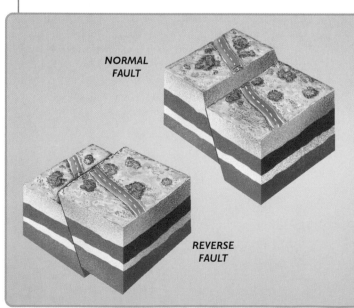

NORMAL FAULT

REVERSE FAULT

FAULTS

When rocks are put under great strain, they sometimes crack. The places where they crack are called **faults**. A normal fault is caused when two blocks of rock are pulled apart, so that one block slips down along the fault plane. When movements in Earth's crust push two blocks of rock together, one of the blocks is forced to move up the fault plane and form a reverse fault.

EARTHQUAKES OF THE WORLD

The red dots on this map of the world shows where serious earthquakes are likely to occur. It looks like a map of the world's main mountain ranges. This is because mountains are formed in areas that are on fault systems or near plate margins. These are unstable areas and are prone to earthquakes. Earthquakes that occur under the sea follow a chain of underwater volcanic mountains.

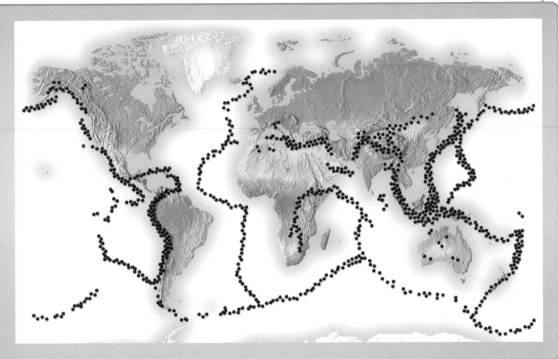

SURFACE WAVES

EPICENTER

BODY WAVES

FOCUS OR HYPOCENTER

◄ FOCUS AND EPICENTER

The **focus**, or hypocenter, of an earthquake is deep underground, at the exact point on a fault where rocks first crack and move. This is where an earthquake starts and where it is strongest. The **epicenter** is the point on Earth's surface directly above the focus. As the body waves move out from the focus toward the surface, however, they often change speed and direction as they pass through different layers and types of rocks. Surface waves travel out in all directions from the epicenter. There are two main kinds of surface waves, named after the scientists who first described them. Rayleigh waves move up and down, while Love waves push rocks from side to side as they travel forward.

EARTHQUAKE DAMAGE

▲ LISBON, PORTUGAL, 1755

On the morning of November 1, 1755, Lisbon was struck by a terrifying earthquake that destroyed buildings and caused a series of huge sea waves to come rushing in from the Atlantic. Overturned lamps started fires that swept through the city and burned for days. Around 60,000 people were killed in the disaster, and **seismologists** have estimated that the original quake might have measured 8.7 on the Richter scale.

Some areas of the world are more likely to experience **earthquakes** than others. The United States, Indonesia and Turkey, for example, are known as active earthquake areas. Japan is situated where four of Earth's plates meet, so it is not surprising that it suffers about one thousand earthquakes every year. In recent times, television has shown the world the devastation that an earthquake can bring, with huge loss of life as well as great damage to property. Seismologists—the scientists who specialize in studying earthquakes—are constantly trying to learn more about them, in the hope that they will be able to predict major **tremors** in the future. They use measuring instruments, called seismometers or seismographs, to measure and record the pattern of **seismic waves** and work out the strength and duration of each earthquake.

THE RICHTER SCALE

The American seismologist Charles F. Richter (1900–85) developed this numbering system in 1935, and it is still the best-known earthquake scale. Each increasing number on the **Richter scale** represents a 10-times increase in the ground movement recorded on a seismometer. So in an earthquake of magnitude 8, for example, the ground shakes 100 times as much as in a magnitude-6 quake.

MAGNITUDE	DESCRIPTION	AVERAGE PER YEAR	INTENSITY NEAR EPICENTER
0–1.9	-	700,000	RECORDED BUT NOT FELT
2–2.9	-	300,000	RECORDED BUT NOT FELT
3–3.9	MINOR	40,000	FELT BY SOME
4–4.9	LIGHT	6,200	FELT BY MANY
5–5.9	MODERATE	800	SLIGHT DAMAGE
6–6.9	STRONG	120	DAMAGING
7–7.9	MAJOR	18	DESTRUCTIVE
8+	GREAT	1 IN 10-20 YEARS	DEVASTATING

SAN FRANCISCO, 1989 ▶

Buildings and roads in San Francisco were damaged during the Loma Prieta earthquake of October 17, 1989. This earthquake measured 7.1 on the Richter scale. The epicenter was near Loma Prieta, about 100 kilometers (60 miles) southeast of San Francisco. It struck at 5:04 P.M., just as a baseball match was about to begin in Candlestick Park. Part of Interstate 880 collapsed, and 62 people lost their lives.

◀ KOBE, JAPAN, 1995

Measuring 7.2 on the Richter scale, the Kobe earthquake on January 17, 1995 killed 5,500 people, devastated the city, and collapsed the Hanshin Expressway in Osaka.

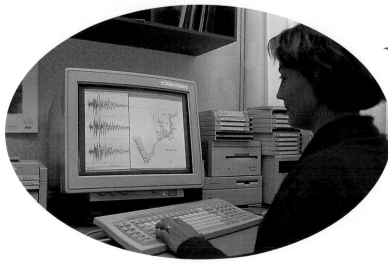

◀ SEISMOMETER INTERPRETATION

Readings from seismometers placed in earthquake regions can be fed directly back to a local laboratory or to laboratories on the other side of the world. Computers are used to interpret the graphs and to assess the size and magnitude of earthquakes. This enables seismologists to build up a pattern of tremors and predict future quakes. People are able to prepare themselves with daily drills and develop technology to build structures that are earthquake resistant.

SEE ALSO	
Earthquakes	**pages 22–23**
Volcanoes	**pages 26–27**

VOLCANOES

A **volcano** is an opening in Earth's crust, where molten rock and gas come from deep underground in Earth's upper **mantle**. Streams of the molten rock— called **magma** within the mantle and **lava** when it reaches Earth's surface— burst through the opening, usually with great force. Sometimes lava flows out quietly, but volcanoes often explode with great violence when they erupt. Most volcanoes are located at or near the world's **plate** boundaries. They occur both on land and under the sea, where plates push together or pull apart. When a volcano has not erupted for thousands of years, it is said to be dormant, or "sleeping." Dormant volcanoes often give off steam or have lava bubbling near the surface, and they may well become active again. Active volcanoes may erupt at any time, and there are more than 1,500 of these in the world.

ASH CLOUD

LAVA FLOW

CRATER

HARDENED LAVA

CENTRAL VENT

SIDE VENT

MAGMA
CHAMBER

MAGMA

RING OF FIRE

The world's active volcanoes are shown here in blue. Many of them lie in a huge belt around the Pacific Ocean. This belt is known as the **Ring of Fire,** and it runs along the edge of the huge Pacific plate. The American part of the Ring of Fire runs from Alaska down the length of the west coast to the Andes mountains. On the other side of the ocean, it runs from Japan down through the islands of Southeast Asia to New Zealand. Many of the Ring's volcanoes are on land, near where the oceanic plate is forced beneath a continental plate.

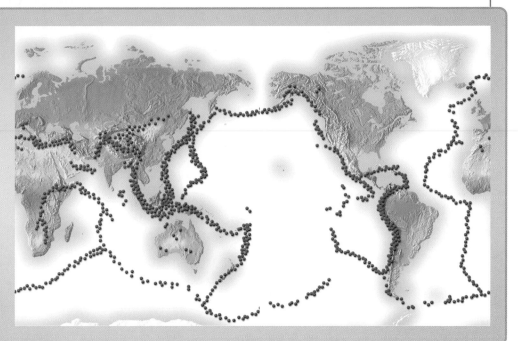

◀ INSIDE A VOLCANO

This cross-section of an erupting volcano shows red-hot magma blasting up through an opening in Earth's crust. The opening is called a vent, and smaller side vents lead off from the main opening. Layers of lava harden beside the central vent, forming a cone-shaped mountain that builds up with each eruption. After an eruption, the vents may be plugged as the magma left within the volcano cools and hardens. When a violent eruption blasts the plug from a vent, it leaves behind a bowl-shaped crater.

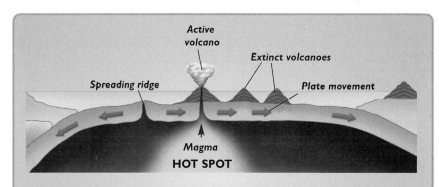

HOT SPOTS

A **hot spot** is a very hot part of Earth's mantle, far away from a plate boundary. The hot spot beneath the crust remains stationary, but the plate above it slowly moves. Every so often, the hot spot burns its way through the moving plate, creating a line of volcanoes. The Hawaiian islands are a good example of this process.

TYPES OF VOLCANO

Volcanoes display different characteristics depending on the conditions in which they erupt. They generally fall into five categories.

PLINIAN

*Gas-rich **magma** explodes inside the mountain, firing the lava up to 30 kilometers (19 miles) in the air.*

HAWAIIAN

After a low-pressure eruption, huge amounts of hot lava flood out to settle in long flows.

STROMBOLIAN

Frequent low-pressure eruptions eject lava blocks mixed with gases.

PELÉAN

Gas-rich magma explodes under low pressure, causing the lava to flow like an avalanche.

VULCANIAN

Periodic higher-pressure explosions send red-hot lava high into the sky, creating large ash clouds.

VOLCANIC FORMS

Volcanoes come in a wide variety of forms and can be classified according to the nature of their eruptions. Both the shape of a volcano and its kind of eruption depend mainly on the type of **lava** that comes out of it. Runny, liquid lava may travel a long way from the vent before it hardens. This kind of flow forms a volcano with gently sloping sides, called a shield volcano. If the lava hardens before it can flow very far, it builds up high layers. Cone-shaped volcanoes often have layers of ash on top and are known as cinder cones or ash-cinder volcanoes. Sometimes lava is thrown up into the air to make spectacular fire fountains. Other volcanoes fling out chunks of solid lava known as pyroclasts. Volcanic activity in a region can also result in features such as **geysers**, hot springs, and mud pots.

GEYSERS ▶

With all its underground heat and activity, a volcanic landscape sometimes needs to let off a little steam. Gases may escape from the ground through vents called fumaroles. When there is water underground, it is heated to boiling point. It then erupts as jets of steam and water called geysers. Geysers may "blow" in this way at regular intervals.

▲ MUD POTS

In volcanic regions, water heated underground can release steam that forces its way to the surface through layers of ash and mud. As the steam leaks through the mud, often bringing volcanic gases and rock fragments with it, it causes the mud to bubble and plop. These mud pots (above) are in Wyoming.

CALDERAS

Large volcanic **craters** are called calderas. These are often formed when a massive blast empties a volcano's magma chamber and causes the volcano to collapse in on itself. Sometimes rain then fills the caldera to form a circular lake, such as Crater Lake in Oregon. This lake formed when rain and melting snow filled the crater of Mount Mazama thousands of years ago.

▲ HOT SPRINGS

Hot springs occur where magma beneath the surface heats up water in cracks in the overlying rock, as happens at Mammoth Hot Springs in Yellowstone National Park (above). The water forms hot springs at the surface. Sometimes the water is warm, and provides a relaxing pool to bathe in. Sometimes the water is too hot for bathing. Hot groundwater can also be used as a source of geothermal power, to drive turbines and generate electricity. As the water cools, minerals dissolved in it may be deposited in layers around the vent. This can form spectacular terraces. Yellow crystals of sulfur form as sulfurous volcanic gases cool.

SEE ALSO

Earth's Changing Surface	**pages 18–19**
Volcanoes	**pages 26–27**

VOLCANOES OF THE WORLD

▲ MONTSERRAT, CARIBBEAN, 1997

On November 4, 1997, a thick mass of red-hot ash, lava fragments, and gases flowed quickly down from Chance Peak, on the Caribbean island of Montserrat. This kind of hot avalanche is known as a **pyroclastic flow**. In this case, the flow was accompanied by an ash cloud that climbed 10 kilometers (6 miles) into the sky.

There have been many famous **volcanic eruptions**. The best documented are those with the highest loss of life. However, many others have occurred in areas where population was small, or before records were kept. Loss of life and damage to land and property are only partly caused as a result of ash, lava, and other erupted material. Very often, mudflows and **tsunamis** are even more devastating. These are often sparked by earthquakes, which themselves are triggered by a volcanic eruption. Some eruptions are completely unexpected, or are much more severe than expected. Other eruptions are predictable. They occur at definite intervals, letting off pressure and releasing hot liquid lava almost continuously.

▲ MOUNT PINATUBO, PHILIPPINES, 1991

Mount Pinatubo, on the island of Luzon in the Philippines, erupted on June 15, 1991. It had been dormant for more than six hundred years. Large quantities of ash and **magma** were erupted. The ash covered the U.S. Chark air base and darkened the skies. The eruption released a great deal of sulfur dioxide into the **atmosphere**, and rock fragments shot 35 kilometers (22 miles) into the air. More than 500 people were killed. Although almost 150 meters (500 feet) of the volcano was blasted away by the eruption, it was a minor eruption compared with those on the island 35,000 years ago. Then the eruption covered the sides of the volcano with more than 100 meters (325 feet) of lava and ash.

◄ MOUNT ST. HELENS, WASHINGTON, 1980

On May 18, 1980, triggered by an **earthquake** measuring 5.1 on the Richter scale, the bulge on the northern flank of the volcano started to move. It resulted in the largest known **landslide** in historic time. The lateral blast as the volcano erupted blew the top 396 meters (1,300 feet) off the mountain. The blast area covered more than 390 square kilometers (150 square miles) and sent thousands of tons of ash into the atmosphere. Glaciers and snow were melted by the hot ash. Trees were felled by the blast, and more than twenty years after the eruption, the vegetation in some areas has still not recovered.

MOUNT UNZEN, JAPAN, 1991 ►

Volcanoes affect many people. Countries have very different cultures, and differing capabilities for scientific study and surveillance. As a result, there are varied public responses to a dangerous volcano. In Japan, the likelihood of a volcanic eruption is high. Schoolchildren learn of the dangers and practice how they should react in an emergency. The eruption of Mount Unzen in 1991 was predicted by scientists and, because those in danger were evacuated, there was very little loss of life. Volcanic ash fell over a wide area but that didn't stop local people going on with their daily lives, like these children going to school in their face masks.

◄ MOUNT FUJI, JAPAN

The sacred mountain of Mount Fuji, Japan's highest peak at 3,776 meters (12,388 feet), is a dormant volcano. It last erupted in 1707, when it scattered ash as far as Tokyo. The mountain looks particularly peaceful, but this dormant appearance can be deceptive, and plumes of smoke are sometimes seen at the summit.

MOUNTAIN BUILDING

▲ APPALACHIANS

This range runs for almost 2,000 kilometers (1,250 miles), from Maine down to Alabama. The highest peak is Mount Mitchell, which is 2,037 meters (6,683 feet) high. But the mountains were much higher after they were formed, up to three hundred million years ago. Their peaks have been gradually worn away by the forces of **erosion** until they are low, round, and smooth.

Mountains form in several different ways, but they are all based on the movement of the rocks that make up the Earth's **tectonic plates**. As the plates push against each other, they buckle at the edges and push mountains up. If the **crust** cracks and forms **faults**, it can have the same effect. When molten rock bursts through the crust, the resulting **volcano** can build a mountain. Some mountains are solitary peaks, standing high above the surrounding landscape. Most, however, are joined together to form a line or series. We call this series of mountains a range, and when ranges are grouped together, they form a chain. The longest and highest ranges, such as the Andes in South America and the Himalayas in Asia, form huge mountain systems.

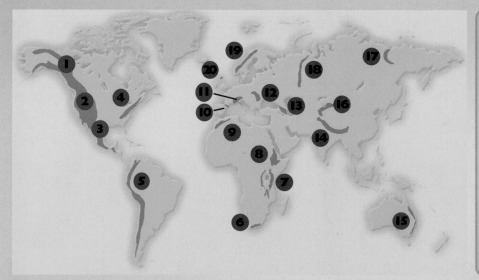

KEY

MOUNTAIN RANGES

1.	Mackenzie Mts	12.	Carpathian Mts
2.	Rocky Mts	13.	Caucasus Mts
3.	Sierra Madre	14.	Himalayas
4.	Appalachians	15.	Great Dividing range
5.	Andes		
6.	Drakensberg Mts	16.	Tien Shan
7.	East African Rift Valley	17.	Verkhoyansk Range
8.	Ethiopian Highlands	18.	Urals Mts
		19.	Scandinavian Highlands
9.	Atlas Mts		
10.	Pyrenees	20.	Scottish Highlands
11.	Alps		

MAJOR RANGES

The two longest mountain ranges in the world are the Andes at 7,200 kilometers (4,475 miles) and the Rockies at 4,800 kilometers (2,980 miles). Together they form a great mountain system known as the Cordilleras, which runs down the Pacific coast of two continents and forms part of the Ring of Fire (see page 27). The third longest range, the Himalayas at 3,800 kilometers (2,360 miles), is the highest and contains the ten tallest peaks in the world.

MOUNTAIN TYPES

There are four main types of mountains, named after the way in which they are formed.

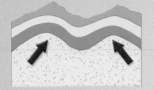

FOLD

As layers of rock are pushed together, they buckle and fold. Mountains form at upfolds, and valleys at downfolds.

DOME

Heat from molten rock pushes top layers of solid rock upward, creating a bulging surface.

FAULT

Layers of rock on one side of a fault, or crack, are pushed upward to form a mountain.

VOLCANIC

Erupting **lava** and ash settle in layers to form a cone-shaped mountain.

▲ ON TOP OF THE WORLD

Most of the world's highest mountains are in the Himalayas, which stretch in a wide curve across the border between India and China, through Bhutan and Nepal to northern Pakistan. The highest peak of all is Mount Everest, which lies on the border between Nepal and Tibet, and reaches up to 8,848 meters (29,028 feet) above sea level. It was first climbed in 1953. Since then many expeditions of mountaineers have reached the summit, such as this group in 1988.

LIFE OF A MOUNTAIN

The jagged peaks of young mountains are worn away by rain, snow, and ice. Gradually the shape of the mountain changes. The outline becomes more rounded and less jagged. Older mountains are smoother and not as high as they once were. Eventually all evidence of a mountain may be removed, leaving a flat landscape.

YOUNG MOUNTAIN RANGE

Young mountains may have sharp, jagged peaks. The Himalayas, Alps, Rockies, and Andes are relatively young mountains. They are less than 70 million years old.

WEARING AWAY

Mountains are attacked by wind, rain, and ice, and their jagged peaks are gradually worn down by erosion over millions of years.

OLD MOUNTAIN RANGE

Weathering *and erosion have smoothed and rounded the peaks. The Appalachians, Urals, and the Highlands of Scotland are more than 250 million years old.*

PEAKS AND VALLEYS

As land is uplifted and mountains form, valleys are also created. These are the low-lying areas of land between mountains and hills. Most valleys are created by rivers. Water flowing down a mountain side often forms a river valley as it carries rock and sediment from the mountain down to the sea. The steeper the slope, the faster a river flows and the deeper it gouges out the valley. Ice moving through a valley in the form of a **glacier** scoops out rock and enlarges the valley. The shape of the valley bottom depends on how the valley was formed. The underlying rocks also affect its shape. The harder rocks may form steep cliffs and waterfalls, while softer rocks are more easily washed away, giving a more rounded valley bottom.

◀ GRAND CANYON

The deep gorges of Grand Canyon in Arizona have been cut out by the running water of the Colorado River, which flows along the bottom of the Canyon. In places, the river is 1.6 kilometers (1 mile) below the tops of the cliffs on either side. During the last million years, ground movements have also lifted the cliffs upward as the river carved deeper into Earth. The landscape reveals a layered history spanning more than 60 million years. **Canyons** are sometimes called ravines or gorges.

VALLEY TYPES

Scientists have named different types of valleys according to their shape and the way in which they were formed.

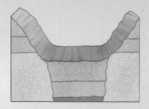

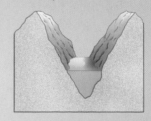

V-SHAPED

A narrow, steep-sided V-shaped valley is carved out by a river flowing through it. Rock layers that make up the sides of the valley are worn away by the water.

U-SHAPED

A broad U-shaped valley is carved out from an existing V-shaped river valley by a glacier moving slowly through it. The glacier deepens and widens the valley, smoothing up the sides in the process.

RIFT VALLEY

*A trough-shaped **rift valley** is formed when a block of rock layers sinks between two **faults** in Earth's **crust**.*

FJORD

*A **fjord** is a deep, narrow sea inlet that was originally carved out by a glacier. During the last ice age, many such valleys were created. After the ice melted, the sea level rose and flooded the resulting fjords.*

FORMATION OF A U-SHAPED VALLEY

When a mountain glacier (see page 57) moves downhill, it follows the path of valleys. These are often V-shaped river valleys. A glacier takes up the whole floor of the valley. As a glacier moves, it collects and carries loose stones and rocks. The glacier and the rocks gouge out the valley floor, so that its shape changes to a U-shape. In a U-shaped valley, there are often piles of rocks, called moraine, left by the glacier that formed it. Where the glacier ended, there are piles of rocks called terminal moraine. The bedrock of the valley may show scratch marks, called striations. These are scrapes made by the rocks carried in the glacier. Smaller glaciers flow into the main glacier from the side. When the glaciers melt, the end of the side glacier is sometimes left hanging high above the main valley. This forms a so-called hanging valley, where running water forms waterfalls.

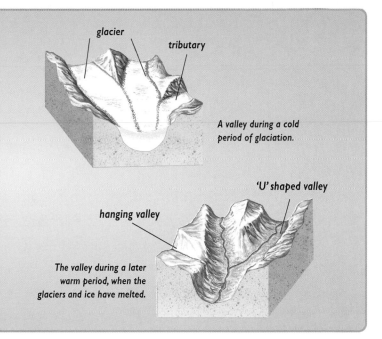

glacier
tributary

A valley during a cold period of glaciation.

'U' shaped valley
hanging valley

The valley during a later warm period, when the glaciers and ice have melted.

◄ THE SNOW LINE

High mountains have snow on the peaks all year round. Above a certain height, called the snow line, there is always a layer of snow on the slopes of a mountain. No plants grow above this line because it is too cold. Near the Equator, where the general climate is warm, the snow line is high up. This is because warm air soon melts any snow falling on the lower slopes. Closer to the poles, where the climate is cold, the snow line is lower.

◄ CASCADE RANGE

The Cascade Range is a chain of volcanic mountains stretching for about 1,100 kilometers (700 miles) from northern California to British Columbia in Canada. Warm, moist air moving in from the Pacific Ocean rises as it reaches the mountains. As it rises, it cools and releases moisture as rain or snow on higher ground and peaks. Rainfall in the Cascades is heavy, and there are many streams and waterfalls. These streams have forged deep valleys in the rock.

SEE ALSO

| Mountain Building | Pages 32-33 |
| Ice | Pages 56-57 |

ROCKS

Rocks make up the hard, solid mass of Earth's **crust**. They are all made of solid chemical substances called **minerals**. Some minerals are made of large **crystals**—solid forms with a regular, geometrical shape—that can be seen easily. Other rocks are made of minerals with crystals so small that the rocks look dense and do not appear to be made up of particles at all. Mountains and cliffs are large masses of rock, while stones, pebbles and grains of sand are all small pieces of rock. There are three main groups of rocks, which are named according to how they were formed. These groups of rocks are called **igneous**, **sedimentary** and **metamorphic**, and they are all involved in different ways in the formation of Earth's crust (see also pages 38–41).

▲ ROCKY LANDSCAPES

In many places, Earth's rocks are covered by soil, which contains tiny bits of rock. The type of rock beneath the surface may affect the kind of plants that grow in a particular region. Sometimes a change in vegetation can be a sign to a geologist that there is a boundary between rock types under ground. This rock face in New Zealand shows the soil is a very thin layer and so only grasses can take root and grow. Underneath are layers of sedimentary rock.

COMMON MINERALS FOUND IN THE THREE ROCK GROUPS

Minerals are the building blocks of rocks. Some minerals, such as quartz, form in all three rock groups. Other minerals, such as the mineral garnet, form only in metamorphic rocks.

IGNEOUS ROCKS	SEDIMENTARY ROCKS	METAMORPHIC ROCKS
Quartz	Quartz	Quartz
Feldspar	Feldspar	Feldspar
Mica	Clay minerals	Mica
Pyroxene	Calcite	Garnet
Amphibole	Dolomite	Pyroxene
Olivine	Gypsum	Staurolite
	Halite	Kyanite

THE ROCK CYCLE

The rocks that make up Earth's crust are constantly changed and rearranged, and this process forms a continuous cycle. When **volcanoes** erupt, they throw out **lava**, or molten rock, onto Earth's surface (**1**). This cools and hardens as igneous rock (**2**). Underground, magma cools very slowly to form igneous rock. Over many years the igneous rock that reaches the surface is eroded by the weather (**3**). Rivers carry the eroded fragments of rock to the ocean, where they settle on the seabed (**4**). There the fragments pile up and settle into layers. As more sediment settles on top, pressure on the lower layers turns them into sedimentary rock (**5**). This process of hardening into rock is called **lithification**. When igneous or sedimentary rocks are subjected to great heat or pressure, their minerals can change and turn them into metamorphic rocks (**6**). Heat inside the Earth melts some rocks, so that they become magma again (**7**), which may come to the surface in **volcanic eruptions** or cool to form igneous rock. The rock cycle is never-ending.

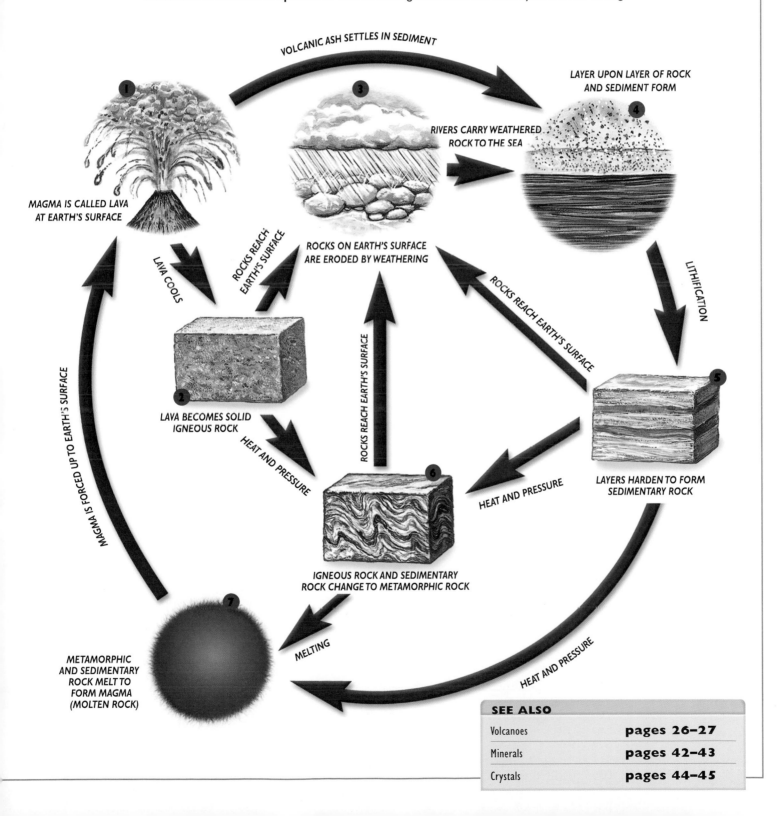

VOLCANIC ASH SETTLES IN SEDIMENT

LAYER UPON LAYER OF ROCK AND SEDIMENT FORM

RIVERS CARRY WEATHERED ROCK TO THE SEA

MAGMA IS CALLED LAVA AT EARTH'S SURFACE

LAVA COOLS

ROCKS REACH EARTH'S SURFACE

ROCKS ON EARTH'S SURFACE ARE ERODED BY WEATHERING

ROCKS REACH EARTH'S SURFACE

LITHIFICATION

MAGMA IS FORCED UP TO EARTH'S SURFACE

LAVA BECOMES SOLID IGNEOUS ROCK

HEAT AND PRESSURE

ROCKS REACH EARTH'S SURFACE

HEAT AND PRESSURE

LAYERS HARDEN TO FORM SEDIMENTARY ROCK

IGNEOUS ROCK AND SEDIMENTARY ROCK CHANGE TO METAMORPHIC ROCK

MELTING

METAMORPHIC AND SEDIMENTARY ROCK MELT TO FORM MAGMA (MOLTEN ROCK)

HEAT AND PRESSURE

SEE ALSO	
Volcanoes	**pages 26–27**
Minerals	**pages 42–43**
Crystals	**pages 44–45**

SEDIMENTARY ROCKS

Sedimentary rocks are formed from particles of other rocks. The weather breaks down rocks into particles, which are then carried away by ice, water, and wind. They are deposited in rivers, lakes and oceans. Over thousands of years, layers of particles, called **sediment**, build up on top of one another. They are squeezed together and gradually harden into rock. Sand particles form sandstone, mud turns into mudstone, and so on. Geologists study fragments and fossils within sedimentary rocks to find out about Earth at the time the rocks were formed. They look particularly at the shape and size of the grains that make up the rock, as well as any fossils that it may contain.

LAYER ▶ UPON LAYER

The layers of sedimentary rocks can be seen on the edge of this hill, where the slope is too steep for any plants to grow. When the rock formed, sediments were laid down on top of one another to form horizontal layers. The layers have been turned on their sides as the rocks have been uplifted by movements deep inside the Earth.

CHALK ▶

Chalk cliffs, such as the famous White Cliffs of Dover on the southern coast of England, are made up of layers of sedimentary rock. Chalk is a form of limestone that is made up mainly of the shells and skeletons of tiny sea animals. Some chalk deposits in Kansas contain the remains of extinct sea creatures, flying reptiles, birds, and fishes. Since chalk is a soft rock, it is easily worn away by the sea.

◄ WEATHERED SANDSTONE

Sandstone is formed from grains of sand held together by fine-grained material, called **matrix**, that acts as a cement. If the matrix holds the sand grains loosely, the sandstone is easily worn away. Weathering has shaped these sandstone rocks in the region of Navajo national monument, in Arizona. Flash floods have scoured away the rocks, which have also been worn away by sand and dust carried by hot, dry winds. Horizontal layers of sandstone occurred as new layers formed and were laid down on top. Such layering is characteristic of sedimentary rock.

▲ CONGLOMERATE

Conglomerate is a sedimentary rock that is made up of rounded pebbles. These are held together with a solid matrix (cement) of pebbles and sand. If the fragments are angular then the rock is called breccia.

SEE ALSO	
Rocks	**pages 36–37**
Weathering and Erosion	**pages 50–51**

IGNEOUS ROCKS

▲ VOLCANIC ASH

The igneous rocks of the Canary Islands were formed by erupting volcanoes. They are made mainly of extrusive igneous rocks. We can see layers of rock and ash from the eruptions as steps on the side of the mountain. Erosion and weathering transport the ash downhill where lush green trees grow in the fertile volcanic soil.

When **magma** cools and hardens, it forms the rocks that we call igneous (which means "fiery"). There are two kinds of **igneous rocks**—intrusive and extrusive. **Intrusive igneous rocks** form underground, when magma cools slowly and turns into solid rock. They are exposed on Earth's surface when the rocks above them wear away. **Extrusive igneous rocks**, on the other hand, are formed when magma cools and solidifies above ground. They are volcanic rocks, spewed from **volcanoes** as **lava**. Extrusive rocks cool faster and their **crystals** are smaller, while intrusive rocks cool more slowly and have larger, coarser grains.

◄ INTRUSIVE ROCK

Granite (left) is the most common kind of intrusive igneous rock found on the Earth's surface. Since it cooled slowly under ground, it has coarse grains. As the overlying sediments wore away, the granite came to the surface. The distinctive cracks in the rock formed as it cooled and the weight of overlying sediments was removed. There are many different types of granite, including coarse-grained pegmatite and fine-grained aplite.

EXTRUSIVE ROCK ►

More than three quarters of all extrusive igneous (or volcanic) rocks are kinds of basalt. The rapid cooling process produces characteristic six-sided columns, such as these basalt structures *(right)* in the Valley of the Organ Pipes, Namibia. Basalt often has such fine grains that they can only be seen under a microscope.

METAMORPHIC ROCKS

Metamorphic rock is sedimentary or igneous rock that has been altered by heat, pressure, or both. The **minerals** and textures of a rock are altered by chemical reactions, turning one type of rock into another. This process is called metamorphism. In most cases, this occurs when rocks meet heat from volcanic activity or through the enormous pressures of mountain building. The minerals that result from the change tell geologists about the temperatures and pressures at which the rock formed. One original type of rock can turn into several different new types. The sedimentary rocks shale and mudstone, for example, can become slate, gneiss, or schist (see page 42), depending on the conditions at the time.

▲ MARBLE

The metamorphic rock marble is often used as a material for sculpture. It is a changed form of the sedimentary rock limestone. Like other metamorphic rocks, marble is formed by heat and pressure in Earth's crust. These forces cause the limestone to change in texture and makeup in a process known as recrystallization. Pure marble is white. When minerals are present during recrystallization, the resulting marble has colored stripes.

▲ GNEISS

Gneiss is a metamorphic rock with large, coarse crystals (see page 44) arranged in light and dark bands. Gneiss often has a stripy appearance. Most of the minerals in gneiss are quartz and feldspar, between bands of mica. Gneiss may form from both igneous and sedimentary rocks.

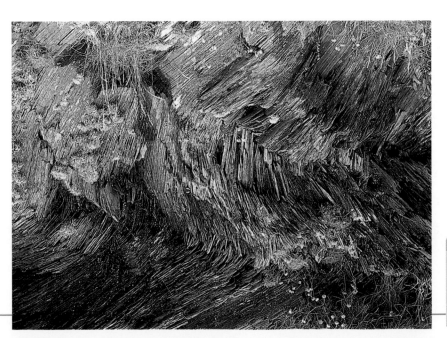

◀ SLATE

Slate is formed from a sedimentary rock such as shale or mudstone. Clay and quartz crystals are changed by a rise in temperature and by pressure into mica. The mica crystals form thin flat layers, which split easily.

MINERALS

MOHS' SCALE OF HARDNESS

Friedrich Mohs (1773–1839) was a German mineralogist (someone who studies minerals). In 1812 he devised a table designed to show the hardness of minerals. There are ten minerals in **Mohs' scale**. Each one can scratch a mark in minerals with lower numbers on the scale. Starting with the softest mineral, they are:

MINERAL	COMMON EQUIVALENT
1. talc	
2. gypsum	fingernail
3. calcite	copper coin
4. fluorite	iron nail
5. apatite	knife blade
6. feldspar	glass
7. quartz	steel file
8. topaz	
9. corundum	
10. diamond	

The solid chemical substances that we call **minerals** are present in all rocks. They occur naturally and form the building blocks of the rocks that make up Earth's **crust**. There are about 3,500 different kinds of minerals, but only about 100 of them are very common. Different rocks contain varying proportions of one or more minerals. The main rock-forming minerals include augite, calcite, feldspar, hornblende, mica, olivine, and quartz. Light-colored rocks that contain quartz are called felsic rocks, while dark-colored rocks that do not contain quartz are called mafic. As well as being different in color and **luster** (see page 43), minerals vary in other properties, such as weight, hardness, and the way in which they break.

MICA SCHIST ▶

Schist is a **metamorphic rock**. It contains the minerals quartz and mica. During the process of metamorphism, the quartz and mica are separated into thin layers, which can form a pattern of wavy stripes. Some forms of mica schist contain the mineral garnet.

Pink feldspar

Quartz

Black tourmaline

◀ **GRANITE**

Granite is one of the best-known rocks, containing quartz, feldspar, and mica. They are clearly recognized by their different colors and shapes. Here, the quartz and feldspar are light in color, and the mica is dark. The **crystals** are large, and can easily be seen.

QUARTZ ➤

Quartz is probably the most commonly occurring mineral and certainly one of the best known. It is a form of silica, and its chemical name is silicon dioxide. Quartz pebbles are commonly found on river beds, and many beaches have quartz sand. It often has a light, milky color, with a white streak and a glassy luster. Some colored varieties of quartz crystals are used as gemstones. These include violet amethyst, pink rose quartz, and yellow citrine. Quartz registers 7 on Mohs' scale and so it is a relatively hard mineral.

◄ CALCITE

Calcite is a common rock-forming mineral made up of calcium carbonate. It is usually white and is soft (registering 3 on Mohs' scale). Calcite occurs in **igneous**, **sedimentary**, and metamorphic rocks. Most forms of sedimentary limestone consist largely of this mineral. Calcite dissolves easily in slightly acidic water, and this is the reason why caves are so often found in limestone regions *(see page 63)*.

CLEAVAGE AND FRACTURE

Different minerals tend to cleave, or split apart, in a particular way and in one or more directions. A mineral's **cleavage** depends on its internal atomic structure, and a split usually occurs along a line of weakness. The split leaves one or more flat surfaces called cleavage planes. Minerals such as mica cleave in one direction, while feldspar cleaves in two directions, and halite in three. Flourite cleaves in four directions—all four corners break away to leave a diamond shape. A **fracture** is an uneven break that leaves jagged edges or splintery pieces.

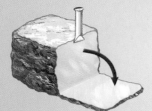

ONE DIRECTION (eg. mica)

TWO DIRECTIONS (eg. feldspar)

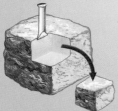

THREE DIRECTIONS (eg. halite)

FOUR DIRECTIONS (eg. flourite, where each corner cleaves away to leave a diamond shape)

▲ EVAPORITES

Evaporites are mineral deposits that are formed when water evaporates. When salt water evaporates, it leaves behind the minerals that were dissolved in it. The main mineral is halite, or rock salt (the chemical name is sodium chloride). This happens naturally when salt lakes dry up, and salt can be collected using shallow, man-made salt pans *(above)*. Rock salt can also be mined from underground deposits, which formed millions of years ago in salt water which evaporated.

CRYSTALS

When we are learning about different animals, we try to sort them into groups, such as mammals, insects, and birds. We do the same with crystals. Each crystal can be classified into a group by looking at the shape of the crystal and finding its symmetry. A crystal's symmetry is found by drawing a number of imaginary lines through the crystal, called lines and axes of symmetry. There are seven main crystal symmetry groups, as well as many subgroups.

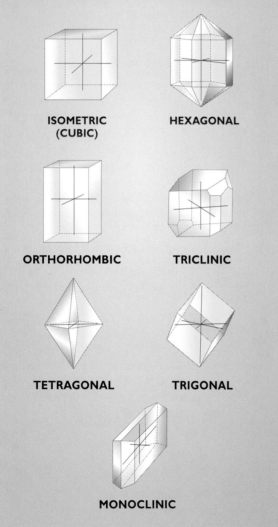

ISOMETRIC (CUBIC)

HEXAGONAL

ORTHORHOMBIC

TRICLINIC

TETRAGONAL

TRIGONAL

MONOCLINIC

Crystals are **minerals** with a regular, geometrical shape. They usually have smooth faces and straight edges, which are caused by a regular arrangement of the atoms that make up the basic building blocks of the mineral. Crystals can be classified, or divided into groups, according to their symmetry. This is their basic geometric shape. They can be further grouped according to their physical properties, such as whether they are heavy or light, rough or smooth. Their optical properties, such as color, may vary. Some crystals are nearly always the same color, while others occur in a range of colors according to their atomic structure. Scientists can also make crystals in a laboratory from their basic chemical ingredients.

AMETHYST ➤

The largest crystals, such as this amethyst from Mexico, are found in geodes, which are cavities in slow-cooling rocks caused by bubbles of volcanic gas. Amethyst is the purple variety of quartz. Other large crystals include beryl and aquamarine. Some examples are up to 2 meters (6 feet) long.

CRYSTAL HABIT

Geologists call the general characteristic appearance and overall shape of a crystal its "habit." Some habits are easily recognizable, such as the three examples below.

SPIKY/ACICULAR CRYSTAL

PRISMATIC CRYSTAL

COLUMNAR CRYSTAL

GROW YOUR OWN ▶

The photograph shows menthol crystals. They have been magnified to make them easier to see. A special type of light has been used for the photograph to make each section a different bright color. The crystals have grown from a variety of starting points. As they have met other crystals growing toward them, the crystals have had to stop growing. In nature, crystal growth is also affected by the amount of space available.

LUSTER

Most crystals are hard and shiny, with flat faces. **Luster** is a surface feature that describes the look of the crystal faces, or the appearance of the mineral. Quartz is an example of a crystal with a vitreous luster, which means that it looks glass-like.

LUSTER	CHARACTERISTICS
Metallic	Strong reflections produced by opaque surfaces
Vitreous	Bright, like glass
Resinous	Characteristic of resins, such as amber
Greasy	The appearance of being coated with an oily substance
Pearly	The whitish, cloudy surface of a material such as pearl
Silky	The smooth sheen of materials such as silk
Adamantine	The brilliant luster of diamonds

SEE ALSO

Minerals	**pages 42–43**
Gemstones	**pages 86–87**

45

FOSSILS

Fossils are the remains of animals or plants that lived on Earth in an earlier geological period. Over millions of years the fossilized remains have been preserved in layers of sedimentary rock. Some have also been preserved in ice, or in sticky pools of tar or resin that hardened over great spans of time. Others are simply traces of footprints or trails left in the rock. Of all the animals and plants that have lived on Earth, only a very small proportion have been preserved as fossils. Nevertheless, those fossils that have survived tell us a great deal about our planet's past and the early history of life on Earth. Scientists called **paleontologists** specialize in finding and studying fossils to learn more about prehistoric animals and plants.

▲ TRILOBITES FOSSIL

About 590 million years ago, some animals developed hard shells. When they died out, their fossils remained, which give today's paleontologists information about the kinds of creatures they were. Hard-shelled trilobites lived from the Cambrian period of geological time to the Permian period *(see pages 14-15)*. They were sea creatures, related to modern shrimps. Trilobites had jointed bodies, many legs, two eyes and a pair of feelers. They were between one centimeter (0.394 inch) and one meter (3.281 feet) long. Trilobite fossils help geologists date rocks. If there is a trilobite fossil in a rock, the rock was formed between 590 million years ago and about 250 million years ago.

◀ STROMATOLITES

Some of the oldest known fossils are stromatolites. They are the remains of mat-like structures that were formed by bacteria. Stromatolites that are more than 3 billion years old have been found on the shores of Australia. Stromatolite mats are still forming in Western Australia.

◄ PREHISTORIC TREES

In prehistoric times, forests were sometimes buried in volcanic ash, mud, and sand. Some of the trees buried in swampy ground were slowly petrified, or turned into stone. All the cells in the tree were replaced by **minerals**, leaving its bark recognizable and rings in the trunk so clear that they can be counted. There are thousands of such fossilized trees in Petrified Forest National Park, Arizona.

▲ STUCK IN TIME

Tree resin is gum-like and sticky, and it can easily trap insects that land on it. Millions of years ago, insects were trapped within the resin of a type of conifer tree that no longer exists today. When the tree died, it became buried, and its resin fossilized and turned into the hard substance that we call amber. The trapped insect looks the same now as it did millions of years ago when it died.

◄ THE FIRST VERTEBRATES

This fossil of a fish gives us a good picture of what the animal looked like. This fish was a vertebrate, meaning that it had a backbone. The details of head, scales, fins, and tail show it was very like some types of modern fish. Fossils tell us that fish first appeared about 450 million years ago, during the Ordovician period.

PROCESS OF FOSSILIZATION

1. Animals or plants that die under water may sink to the floor of the river, lake, or sea. The soft body parts of an animal rot or are eaten by other animals.

2. Only the hard parts, such as the teeth, bones and shell remain. Gradually the remains are buried under layers of sand, mud, and other sediment.

3. Minerals in the water replace the minerals that make up the hard parts of the animal. They become fossils. Where hard parts have rotted, they may leave a space in the sediment that is the same shape as the animal. The minerals may fill this space and create a copy of the shape of the missing animal. This is a fossil cast.

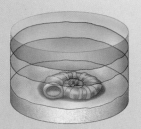

4. The fossil may be buried deeper by further layers of sediment, or it may appear at the surface as rocks are uplifted or when overlying rocks are washed away.

LEARNING FROM FOSSILS

We have learned everything that we know about prehistoric plants and animals from **fossil** finds. An entire prehistoric animal is only rarely found, however, and most fossils consist of bones, teeth or shells. So **paleontologists** have to piece information together from many different sources. When scientists first found dinosaur fossils, they had no idea what they were. Less than two hundred years ago, scientists realized that they were extinct reptiles, and only in 1841 were they given the name dinosaurs, meaning "terrible lizards." Since then paleontologists have used many thousands of finds to put together the picture of prehistoric life that we have today. We now know that dinosaurs lived on Earth for about 165 million years, and died out about 65 million years ago. We cannot be sure why this happened, but most scientists believe that Earth was hit by a giant meteorite. The resulting dust and smoke may have blocked out sunlight for years and killed many plants and animals, including dinosaurs. It is amazing to think that if scientists had not found fossilized bones, we would not even know that dinosaurs ever existed.

AMMONITE FOSSIL ➤

Since many fossils formed in **sediment** on the ocean floor, shellfish fossils are very common. In this fossilized ammonite *(right)*, the animal's shell has been replaced by a **mineral** called iron pyrite, which is also known as "fool's gold." Ammonites lived during the Mesozoic era at the same time as dinosaurs, and they died out at the same time. As an ammonite grew, it added chambers to its shell and lived in the outermost, largest one. Like the shellfish known as a nautilus, which is still alive today, the ammonite moved by changing the amount of air in its chambers.

▲ TRACE FOSSIL

This dinosaur footprint is a trace fossil—something left behind such as a trail, a burrow, or droppings. This particular dinosaur once walked on soft sands that then turned into rock. Studies of footprints give paleontologists an idea of an animal's size and weight.

MARY ANNING

When they were children, Mary Anning and her brother Joe went fossil-hunting on the beach at Lyme Regis in Dorset, England. They sold the fossils they found in their father's shop. Many people enjoyed collecting these strange objects. In 1810, Mary found the fossilized remains of an ichthyosaur in the cliffs of blue lias (a kind of limestone). Later, she discovered two complete plesiosaurs, and the first pterodactyl found in England, as well as many other fossils. Mary Anning continued to fossil hunt until she died in 1847.

WEATHERING AND EROSION

The rocks at the surface of Earth's **crust** are gradually broken down by exposure to the **atmosphere**. The effects of wind, water, and other chemical processes cause rocks to break and decay in an overall process called **weathering**. Weathered rocks may remain in the same position, but usually the fragments are moved downhill or downwind. In this process, which is known as **erosion**, fragments are carried away and deposited elsewhere as **sediment**. Rain, ice, wind, and changes in temperature all contribute to the breakdown and removal of rock particles. Too much water in the soil can cause **landslides**, while wind can gradually wear down mountains and, in deserts, create and move sand dunes. Unlike the dramatic instant effects of **earthquakes** and **volcanoes**, however, weathering and erosion change the appearance of particular landscapes over very long periods of time.

▲ THE POWER OF WATER

Fast-flowing mountain streams can move large fragments of rock downstream. As the streams come together to form larger, slow-moving rivers, the water drops its load of rock fragments. Larger, heavier fragments are dropped first, while finer sediment is carried further downstream, sometimes all the way to the sea. When heavy rainfall causes rivers to flow faster, rocks are carried further and are broken into smaller fragments along the way.

HEAT AND COLD

Repeated changes in temperature can cause "onion skin" weathering in rock. For example, in desert regions temperatures are hot during the day but cold at night. During the day, the heat of the Sun causes the rocks to expand. At night, the intense cold causes the rock to shrink. This regular change in temperature strains the rock and cracks appear. Gradually these cracks expand until part of the rock falls away, giving it the appearance of layers similar to those of an onion. The broken fragments may be eroded by wind or flash floods.

LANDSLIDES

When a hillside becomes unstable, a large mass of rock and soil may move or crash down the slope.

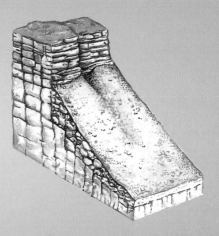

The slow movement of soil downhill is called creep. The effects can only be seen over a long period of time.

When rocks are cracked and broken by water, ice, or heat, blocks may slide vertically to form stepped sections.

When soil is filled up with water after heavy rainfall, rock fragments may break away from the face of the slope and slide quickly downhill.

◄ WEATHERED PINNACLES

The extraordinary shapes of the sandstone pinnacles of Bryce Canyon, in Utah, have been carved over millions of years. This extreme weathering has been caused by the effects of wind, water, and ice. The region is dry in summer, so sand and dust particles are lifted and carried by strong winds.

As the wind batters rocks, the particles wear them away. In winter there is heavy snowfall, and in spring melting water seeps into the rocks and freezes at night.

ICE EFFECTS

When water freezes, it expands (gets bigger). In cold regions and mountainous areas, rain freezes in the cracks and joints of rocks. This gradually pushes the rocks apart. Over time, pieces of the rock break away and fragments fall downhill, leaving a jagged and fractured effect as shown above.

SEE ALSO

| Deserts | pages 54–55 |
| Caves | pages 62–63 |

SOIL AND LANDSCAPES

TYPES OF SOIL

Soil can be divided into four basic types, depending on the minerals and chemicals that it contains.

TEMPERATE FORESTS

The soil beneath broad-leaved forests is very fertile. It has an even brown surface layer. In Europe, there are many well-established forests. They have flourished because of the wet seasons.

TEMPERATE GRASSLANDS

The soil beneath temperate grasslands is deep and dark-colored. The prairies of North America, the steppes of Europe and Asia, the pampas of South America, the savanna of Africa, and the grasslands of India are among the most fertile of all soils.

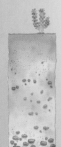

DRY CLIMATE

*Desert soils, such as those in the Sahara, contain almost no organic matter and are very dry. Plants and trees that surround an **oasis** (see page 54) will survive.*

WET TROPICAL RAINFORESTS

Tropical rainforests have a thin but fertile top layer of humus. It is a red or yellow color, and up to 10 meters (33 feet) deep. The clay layer below is infertile. The soil becomes infertile where tropical rainforest is cleared.

As rock is weathered, a layer of loose fragments builds up on top of the underlying, solid bedrock. This layer of weathered material is called the **regolith**, and at its very top is a small surface layer of soil. This is made up of tiny rock particles, sand, and clay, as well as rotting organic matter called **humus**. Microscopic organisms break down the mineral particles within rock fragments to form **soil**. A wet climate is necessary for the chemical reactions needed, and the rate at which soil is made and its thickness depend mainly on a region's climate. It generally takes thousands of years for a thick, fertile soil to develop. The type of soil determines which plants will grow in a region. If the climate is too dry or too wet, the soil gradually becomes barren. Without soil, we would have no food and there would be no life on land.

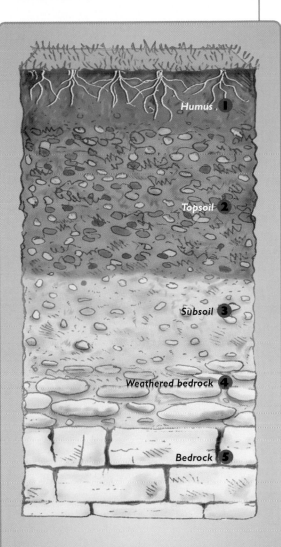

Humus **1**

Topsoil **2**

Subsoil **3**

Weathered bedrock **4**

Bedrock **5**

SOIL PROFILE

A slice of soil, from the surface down to hard rock, is called the soil profile. The layers that make up the profile are called horizons. The number and thickness of the horizons vary with soil type. In the illustration, the top layer (horizon **1**) is a layer of humus. Humus contains living plant roots and animals, such as worms, along with their decaying remains. Topsoil (horizon **2**) is a dark fertile soil, rich in humus. Subsoil (horizon **3**) has little organic matter, but does have minerals that have been washed down from the layers above. Below this is an infertile layer of weathered bedrock (horizon **4**). The lowest layer is solid bedrock (horizon **5**).

▲ PREVENTING EROSION

In many parts of Asia, such as Bali in Indonesia (above), hillsides are cut into terraces to prevent soil **erosion**. A series of steps stops material sliding downhill, and terraces make it easier for farmers to control the flow of rainwater needed to irrigate their crops. Streams are diverted to the terraced fields, where rice and other crops can be grown.

◄ THE DUST BOWL

Rainfall on sandy soil is soon lost, as water drains into the layers beneath. In the 1930s, poor farming methods in the once fertile Great Plains region of North America led to the drying out of the topsoil. The soil was eroded and blew away, leaving the land barren. With no vegetation, the area became a dust bowl (left). A Soil Conservation Service was set up in 1935, and farmers were taught to protect the soil and not overwork it. In addition, many trees were planted to break the force of the winds.

SEE ALSO	
Rocks	**pages 36–37**
Weathering and Erosion	**pages 50–51**

DESERTS

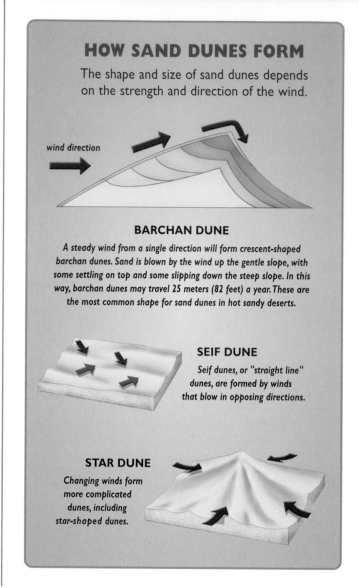

HOW SAND DUNES FORM

The shape and size of sand dunes depends on the strength and direction of the wind.

wind direction

BARCHAN DUNE

A steady wind from a single direction will form crescent-shaped barchan dunes. Sand is blown by the wind up the gentle slope, with some settling on top and some slipping down the steep slope. In this way, barchan dunes may travel 25 meters (82 feet) a year. These are the most common shape for sand dunes in hot sandy deserts.

SEIF DUNE

Seif dunes, or "straight line" dunes, are formed by winds that blow in opposing directions.

STAR DUNE

Changing winds form more complicated dunes, including star-shaped dunes.

Deserts are dry, barren places where very little rain falls. Any region that gets less than ten centimeters (four inches) of rain a year is called a desert. Many deserts are hot, sandy places, like much of the Sahara Desert in Africa. But there are other desert landscapes, including rocky hills and flat, stony plains. In hot deserts, daytime temperatures often reach over 40 °C (104 °F), but fall very fast at night, sometimes to as low as freezing. The two coldest regions on Earth, the Arctic and Antarctic, can also be called deserts. These polar regions are so cold that there is little rainfall and any moisture instantly freezes. Few plants and animals can survive in any desert unless they have adapted to survive with little water and extreme changes in temperature.

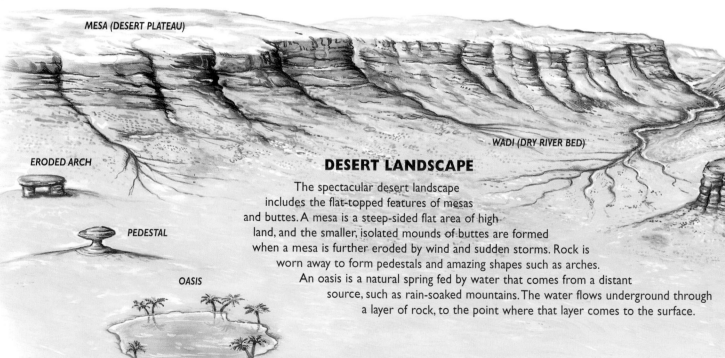

MESA (DESERT PLATEAU)

WADI (DRY RIVER BED)

ERODED ARCH

PEDESTAL

OASIS

DESERT LANDSCAPE

The spectacular desert landscape includes the flat-topped features of mesas and buttes. A mesa is a steep-sided flat area of high land, and the smaller, isolated mounds of buttes are formed when a mesa is further eroded by wind and sudden storms. Rock is worn away to form pedestals and amazing shapes such as arches. An oasis is a natural spring fed by water that comes from a distant source, such as rain-soaked mountains. The water flows underground through a layer of rock, to the point where that layer comes to the surface.

DESERTS OF THE WORLD

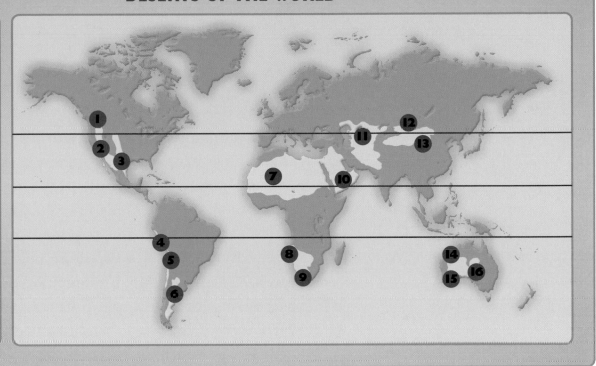

KEY

□ DESERTS

1. Great Basin
2. Mojave
3. Sonoron
4. Peruvian
5. Atacama
6. Patagonian
7. Sahara
8. Namib
9. Kalahara
10. Arabian
11. Karakum
12. Takla Makan
13. Gobi
14. Great Sandy
15. Gibson
16. Simpson

IN THE RAINSHADOW ➤

Rainshadow deserts, such as the Patagonian Desert in Argentina, form behind coastal mountains. The Patagonia lies on the inland side of the Andes Mountains in South America. Warm, moist air from the sea rises as it is blown inland. As it flows over coastal mountains, the air is cooled, clouds form and it rains. Beyond the mountain, the air no longer holds enough water to rain. A dry desert area forms in the shadow of the mountains.

SEA — warm, moist air — COASTAL MOUNTAIN — dry air — DESERT

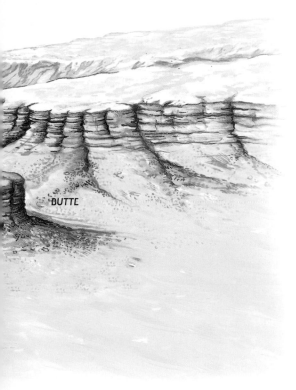

BUTTE

PEDESTALS

Rock is eroded in the desert into all sorts of shapes and sizes. Many have a distinctive mushroom shape, with a wide, round top on a narrow base—this is called a pedestal. The shape is formed by sand and dust. The sand is blown off the surface of the desert, and most of it speeds along close to the ground. This wears away the base of the rock, forming the pedestal.

SEE ALSO

| Weathering and Erosion | pages 50-51 |
| Soil and Landscapes | pages 52-53 |

ICE

▲ FROZEN IN TIME

Ice from the last ice age still exists in places like Greenland and the Antarctic. In Siberia in the Russian Federation scientists have found several woolly mammoths, frozen in ancient ice. Scientists can study these animals, even though they became extinct ten thousand years ago. They tell us the age of the landmass they inhabit. Woolly mammoths were related to modern elephants, but were much bigger. Some were 4.3 meters (14 feet) tall. Their tusks could be 4 meters (13 feet) long. The photo above shows the leg of a woolly mammoth. You can see the wide foot, which worked like a snowshoe, preventing the foot from sinking too deeply into the snow.

About 10 percent of the Earth's land and 12 percent of its oceans are permanently covered with ice. At the two polar regions and in the world's high mountain ranges, huge areas are covered by a layer of ice. In the northern polar region, most of the ice floats on the waters of the Arctic Ocean. Around the South Pole, the ice covers the frozen continent of Antarctica. There, the thickest ice has been measured at more than 4,700 meters (15,400 feet). At times in the past, during intensely cold periods called **ice ages**, even more of the world was covered with ice sheets. During these periods, the **ice caps** built up as more and more snow fell and little or none melted. Masses of ice flowed slowly downhill from high, cold mountains to form the world's **glaciers**.

ICE AGES

During ice ages, more of the world is covered by ice. We are now between ice ages, in what is called an interglacial period. The last ice age ended about 11,500 years ago.

THE ARCTIC TODAY

Arctic ice covers the northern regions of Canada and Russia.

THE ARCTIC 30,000 YEARS AGO

During the last ice age, ice covered all of present-day Canada, northern Europe and most of Russia.

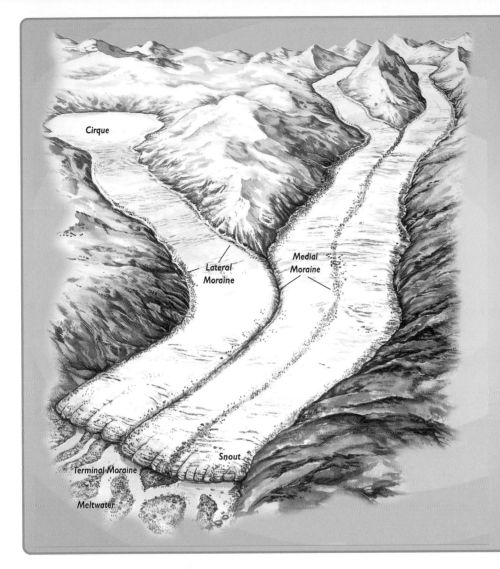

Cirque

Lateral Moraine

Medial Moraine

Snout

Terminal Moraine

Meltwater

ANATOMY OF A GLACIER

Glaciers form on ice caps or in mountains, where more snow falls in winter than is melted in summer. The snow builds up in a small rocky basin called a **cirque**. Eventually, the weight of the snow above squashes air out of the snow underneath and turns it to a kind of snowy ice called **firn**. Under the weight of the ice and snow, the firn ice begins to move downhill as a glacier. In high mountain ranges, glaciers often follow valleys as they make their way downhill. Rocks, boulders, and other debris, called **moraine**, are carried along by the ice and scratch the rock beneath the glacier. Lateral moraine develops at the sides of the glacier, and medial moraine forms down the middle when two glaciers merge. Terminal moraine forms across the front end, or snout, of the glacier. Meltwater usually forms streams in front of the snout. Most glacier ice moves very slowly, traveling less than one meter (3 feet) a day, but the movement of some glaciers in Greenland and Alaska have been measured at more than 20 meters (65 feet) a day.

◄ ICEBERGS

Icebergs are masses of ice floating in the sea. They are much bigger than they look, because only about a seventh of their ice appears above the water. Icebergs break off from glaciers and ice shelves in both the Arctic and Antarctic regions. This large tabular (table-shaped) iceberg was photographed in Antarctica.

SEE ALSO

| Peaks and Valleys | **pages 34-35** |
| Weathering and Erosion | **pages 50-51** |

RIVERS

▲ TYPES OF RIVER

There are three types of rivers, perennial, ephemeral, and seasonal. Perennial rivers flow throughout the year. In tropical and temperate regions the rainfall provides a continuous supply of water to keep the river flowing. All the major rivers of the world, such as the Nile *(above)* and the Amazon, are perennial rivers. Ephemeral rivers are dry for most of the year. Sudden flash floods in desert regions, such as the Namib in southern Africa, fill dry rivers for short periods. Seasonal rivers flow for part of the year. The river beds dry up during the summer, when there is little or no rain. This happens in some of the drier regions of Europe, such as southern Spain.

A **river** is a large body of water that flows in a channel. Rivers start as small streams high up on hills or mountains, carrying water from rain or melted snow. The small streams flow quickly down the steep slopes, and then join together to form a small river. These small rivers often flow together on flatter ground, forming one big, wide river. Much of the rainwater that falls on land drains into the nearest river. The land that a river drains is called its drainage basin. If there is more rainwater than the river can carry in its normal course, the river overflows its banks and floods the surrounding land, which is called the **floodplain**. Rivers go on flowing downhill until they reach the sea. As they do so, they shape the landscape by wearing away rocks and soil and carrying huge amounts of sediment to the sea.

THE WATER CYCLE

Rivers form an important part of a never-ending cycle, carrying water to the world's oceans and seas. The Sun's heat changes some of the water in seas and lakes into vapor. Water vapor from the land also rises into the air and the vapor forms clouds. Cooling clouds release rain, and some of the rainwater forms streams and rivers on land. Then the cycle starts all over again.

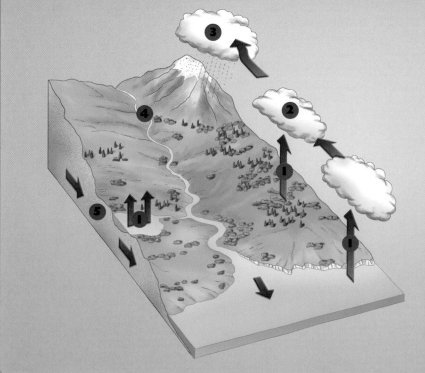

STAGES OF THE WATER CYCLE

1.   *Heat from the Sun turns surface water and water from lakes, rivers and seas into vapor.*

2.   *The higher the vapor rises, the cooler it gets until it turns into ice and forms clouds.*

3.   *Clouds release their water when they get too heavy or too cold. The water then returns to Earth's surface as rain.*

4.   *Rain runs down the mountainsides and into rivers and streams. Some water is absorbed into the soil.*

5.   *The absorbed water travels downhill and back into the sea.*

SOURCE

HEADWATERS

WATERFALL

MEANDERS

OXBOW LAKE

TRIBUTARY

MOUTH

THE COURSE OF A RIVER

The beginning of a river is called its source. Streams flow together to form the river's headwaters. Here the water is shallow and fast-moving. Where the water tumbles down steep slopes or over a cliff, it forms a waterfall. Further on, where the slope is gentler and the wide river moves more slowly, it loops around to form meanders. Sometimes the outside bend of a meander is cut off as the river changes its course, leaving a crescent-shaped body of water called an oxbow lake. Smaller branch rivers, called tributaries, flow into the main river, which reaches the sea at a place called its mouth.

◀ NIAGARA FALLS

Halfway between Lake Erie and Lake Ontario, on the U.S.–Canada border, the Niagara River plunges over a steep gorge. This step in the river creates the Niagara Falls. This famous natural tourist attraction is made up of the American Falls and the Horseshoe Falls *(left)*, which are separated by Goat Island. The greatest drop is about 54 meters (176 feet). The force of the water is used to generate electricity in hydroelectric power stations.

LAKES

A lake is a large body of water that is surrounded by land. Lakes form in hollows in Earth's surface, called **basins**. Lake water comes from rainfall and melting snow, and most lakes are fed by inlet rivers and streams. This means that most lakes are full of fresh water, and they have at least one outlet river flowing out of the basin. A lake without an outlet loses water by evaporation and usually becomes salty. The Caspian Sea, which is the largest lake in the world in terms of surface area, is a salt lake, although its water is less salty than sea water. Its surface covers 371,000 square kilometers (143,250 square miles)—an area larger than New Mexico. Some lakes last for millions of years, but most are fairly short-lived in geological terms. They sometimes dry up or fill with **sediment**, and their remnants form swamps and marshes.

HOW LAKES FORM

Many of the world's lake basins were made by glaciers. Others formed when forces inside Earth caused its surface to move and crack, leaving a space to be filled by water.

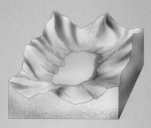

KETTLE LAKE

As a glacier moves downhill, the ice that is left behind settles in small hollows. The hollows are surrounded by rocks and pebbles that have been carried by the glacier. After the ice has melted, the hollow may fill with water to form a kettle lake.

VOLCANIC LAKE

*Volcanic lakes form in the **craters** of extinct or dormant **volcanoes**. When it rains, water fills the crater.*

OXBOW LAKE

An oxbow lake is formed when a bend in the river is cut off from the main flow (see page 59).

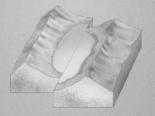

FAULT LAKE

*Movement of rocks on either side of a **fault** may form a low-lying space into which water can drain.*

THE END OF A LAKE

After a few thousand years, lakes may fill up with silt and mud washed in from the surrounding land.

As the lake is filled with sediment, it becomes smaller and shallower.

Islands take shape in the lake, reeds grow, and swamps form.

As the plants grow, the swamp dries out further and finally the lake disappears.

THE GREAT LAKES ▶

The five Great Lakes, on the border between Canada and the United States, contain almost one fifth of the world's freshwater. Lake Superior is the world's largest freshwater lake in terms of area, and it is also the deepest of the Great Lakes. About 200 rivers flow into it, and at its eastern end the lake's waters flow into the St. Mary's River, which links it to Lake Huron. The Great Lakes were formed by **glaciers** about 25,000 years ago. The glaciers scooped out enormous trenches and pushed up piles of rocks. When the glaciers melted, water filled the trenches and the rocks formed a barrier, which stopped the water from draining away.

CANADA

Lake Superior

Lake Huron

UNITED STATES

Lake Michigan

Lake Ontario

TORONTO ●

LANSING ■

DETROIT ●

Lake Erie

■ CHICAGO

◀ LAKE BAIKAL, RUSSIA

Lake Baikal (left), in south-eastern Russia, is the deepest lake in the world—it is 1,620 meters (5,315 feet) at its deepest point. It also holds more water than any other freshwater lake—over one fifth of the world's freshwater and more than the Great Lakes combined. Its surface freezes over each winter. The lake fills a deep **rift valley** that formed about 30 million years ago, making Baikal one of the world's oldest lakes. It has 336 rivers flowing into it, but just one outlet river.

SEE ALSO	
Ice	**pages 56-57**
Rivers	**pages 58-59**

CAVES

Acave is a natural hollow space formed mainly in rock. Some are short, narrow tunnels, while others are huge, deep caverns. Most of the world's caves are found in limestone regions, where rock is dissolved by rainwater over thousands of years. Underground rivers often flow through these caves, speeding up the processes that wear away the rock. In other areas, caves are also formed along coasts, in ice, and in lava.

ICE, SEA, AND LAVA

ICE CAVE

Caves can form in glaciers, icebergs, and ice sheets. They are often hollowed out by water flowing beneath the frozen surface. Ice caves constantly change and rarely last a long time.

SEA CAVE

The pounding action of waves make cracks in coastal cliffs, until pieces of rock break off and a cave forms.

VOLCANIC CAVE

When a volcano's river of lava cools, it sometimes hardens quickly on the outside but stays hot and liquidy on the inside. Lava flows on, and finally drains away to leave a hollow tube. These volcanic caves, called lava tubes, can be more than 10 kilometers (6 miles) long.

▲ STALACTITES AND STALAGMITES

Water flowing over rock dissolves minerals in the rock. The water that drips from the ceiling of a limestone cave carries with it some of the dissolved rock, which includes the mineral calcite. With each drip a little calcite is left behind, gradually forming an icicle-shaped rock. As more calcite is added, the **stalactite** grows slowly towards the floor of the cave. A **stalagmite** forms on the cave floor where the drips land. Scientists can use stalagmites, stalactites, **fossils**, and other remains to find out how old a cave is. The scientific name for stalagmites and stalactites is speleothems.

LIMESTONE CAVE

Limestone often has lines of weakness, joints, and cracks. Carbonic acid, a weak acid found in rainwater, is able to dissolve limestone over time. As the rainwater seeps into the cracks, the carbonic acid dissolves the rock. On the surface this creates a bare, stony surface called a limestone pavement, where the individual slabs of stone are called **clints** and the grooves between them are **grykes**. The water widens cracks, and a stream disappears underground through a **sinkhole**. As more rock is eaten away underground, part of the roof may collapse and leave a large cavern. The water forms underground streams, which carry away the dissolved rock.

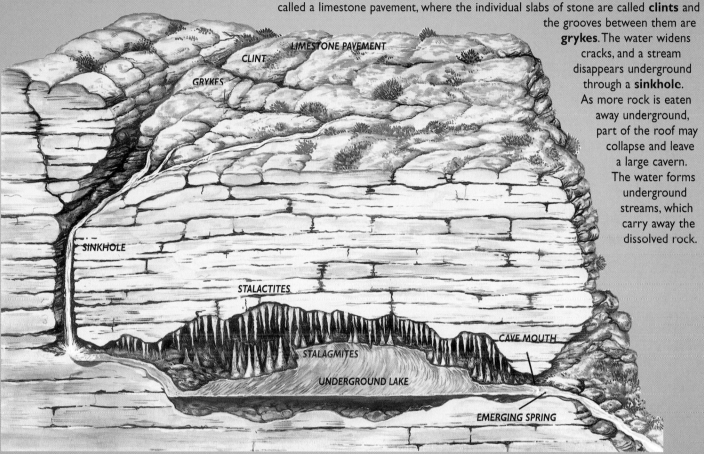

LIMESTONE PAVEMENT

CLINT

GRYKES

SINKHOLE

STALACTITES

STALAGMITES

UNDERGROUND LAKE

CAVE MOUTH

EMERGING SPRING

◀ TOWER KARST

A limestone landscape with many underground caves is called karst (from the name of a region in Slovenia). In the Guilin Hills of southern China (left), the fast erosion of limestone has left steep, narrow pinnacles. This type of landscape is called tower karst, and beneath the hills lies a whole network of caves.

63

COASTLINES

The world's coastlines, where the sea meets the land, show a wide variety of landforms. The shape of the coast depends on many factors, including the action of waves, the strength of the wind, and the type of rock present in a region. All over the world, there is a constant battle between land and sea, as waves pound against the shore. This process creates many different kinds of **beaches**, from palm-fringed strips of flat sand to windswept piles of pebbles and rocks. The amount and type of **sediment**—made up of rock particles, sand, and mud—that is washed down to the sea by rivers also shapes the coastline. The fresh water of a large river meets the salt water of the sea at a broad inlet called an **estuary**. Here, in the partly salty waters, there may be mud flats, salt marshes, and swamps.

◄ **CHESAPEAKE BAY**

Chesapeake Bay is the largest inlet, or coastline opening, on the Atlantic coast of the United States. It is narrow, and about 320 kilometers (200 miles) long. The channel at the entrance to the bay is 19 kilometers (12 miles) wide. Seagoing ships can sail almost the whole length of the bay. The shore is cut by smaller bays and by the wide mouths of several rivers. Salt marshes and swamps have formed in the bay.

PEBBLE BEACH

Pebbles are rock fragments that have been worn down and rounded by **weathering**. Rock fragments are washed down a river from the mountains. They are rolled and polished on their journey. The pebbles on a beach may be made up of only one rock type, all of similar size and shape, or there may be examples of many different rock types. Pebbles may be white, pink, green, and brown, depending on the color of the rocks from which the pebbles were made.

GOLDEN SANDS

Most of the world's tropical beaches have wide expanses of gleaming white sand. Sand is tiny pieces of rock less than 2 millimeters (0.08 inch) across. On white beaches this is mainly made up of the most common mineral, quartz. Seashells are also broken up and worn down to make white grains.

VOLCANIC BEACH

Some of the beaches of Hawaii (right), as well as those in other parts of the world, are mainly made up of small grains of volcanic rock or ash. The main volcanic rocks, such as basalt, are dark-colored. They are eventually worn down into grains of sand. This is why some volcanic beaches have black sand.

BIG SUR, CALIFORNIA

The coastline of California has both rocky cliffs and sandy bays. Cliffs have formed where waves have battered the rock, **eroding** it at beach level. Continual erosion weakens the rock above, and eventually it collapses. The broken rock is washed away, leaving a cliff face behind. Bridges have been built to span the deep gorges and valleys. These valleys have been cut out by rivers or eroded by wind and waves.

65

FORMING COVES

A cove is a small bay or inlet on the coast. It forms in an area of coast that juts out into the sea, called a headland. First the sea wears away a weak spot in the cliff, where the rock is softest. It wears this away further to make a cove. Two coves next to each other may eventually open up to make a larger bay.

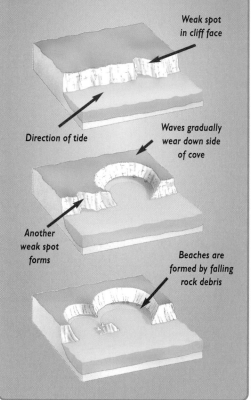

Weak spot in cliff face

Direction of tide

Waves gradually wear down side of cove

Another weak spot forms

Beaches are formed by falling rock debris

CHANGING COASTS

Coastlines are always changing. Beaches are constantly being built up or washed away. The action of waves might even move a beach slowly along a coast. Rocky cliffs are worn away by crashing waves, so that they eventually crumble and fall, sometimes leaving spectacular arches and pillars. At the same time, rock fragments are washed down rivers and may be pushed along the coast by the wind and waves to form a new coastline. Many of these processes take place over a long period of time, but an area of coastline can be changed rapidly by severe storms. Strong, destructive waves may be whipped up by the wind to batter cliffs and carry rocks, pebbles, and sand out to sea. When the weather is calm, waves carry pebbles and sand back up the beach and build up the coast again. These are called constructive waves.

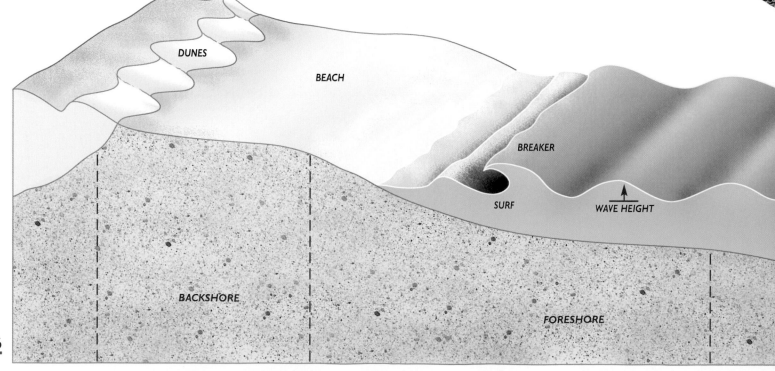

DUNES

BEACH

BREAKER

SURF

WAVE HEIGHT

BACKSHORE

FORESHORE

TIDES

Tides are the movement of sea water towards the land and away from it. Each day there are high tides (when the water comes up the beach) and low tides (when the water covers less of the beach). Tides are caused by the gravity of the Sun and Moon, which pull at the sea water on Earth. This makes the oceans bulge up in a high tide twice a day. When the Sun and Moon are in line, the pull of gravity on Earth is greatest, and the tides are highest. These are called spring tides. When the Sun and Moon pull in opposite directions, there are neap tides. In a neap tide, the change in the water level is only small. Spring and neap tides each happen twice a month.

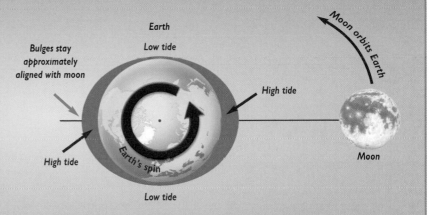

Earth

Low tide

Bulges stay approximately aligned with moon

High tide

Moon orbits Earth

High tide

Earth's spin

Moon

Low tide

◀ STACKS

This tall pillar of rock *(left)*, called a stack, once was joined to the nearby cliff. This is shown clearly by the horizontal layers of rock in the cliff and the stack, which join up exactly if you follow them across. The stack was separated from the cliff by the pounding action of the sea. First it opened up a small cave, which then grew into an arch, and finally left a stack when the top of the arch collapsed.

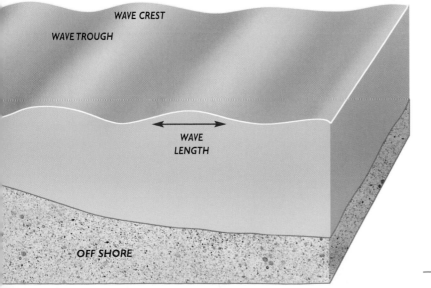

STAGE 1	STAGE 2	STAGE 3
Vertical cracks in the cliff are widened by the action of the sea. Sea caves are formed.	The waves erode the cave even further, enlarging it to form an arch.	The top of the arch collapses, leaving a stack.

◀ WAVES

Most waves are caused by the wind, which makes the surface of the sea rise and fall as it blows. At its height, it is called the wave's crest. At its lowest point, it is called the wave's trough. A gentle breeze produces small waves in both height and length. A strong wind makes large, powerful waves. When a wave reaches the foreshore, it breaks, or collapses. Where the waves break is called the surf. The force of the water when it hits rocks on shore erodes the rocks. As a wave travels, it can pick up sand and pebbles to and from the beach. As the wind blows it also picks up sand and can create sand dunes.

WAVE CREST

WAVE TROUGH

WAVE LENGTH

OFF SHORE

SEE ALSO	
Weathering and Erosion	**pages 50–51**
Coastlines	**pages 64–65**

▲ SALT WATER

The sea tastes salty because it contains the dissolved mineral sodium chloride, or salt (above). Most seawater has a salt content of about 3.5 percent, which is twice as salty as human tears. The other 96.5 percent is made up of fresh water, which contains hydrogen and oxygen. Along with salt, there are small amounts of other ingredients, such as sulfur, magnesium, calcium, and potassium. The saltier the water, the easier it is to float in.

OCEANS OF THE WORLD

More than 70 percent of the Earth's surface is covered by water. Only 3 percent of this water is contained in rivers and lakes. The rest is contained in the salty waters of the world's oceans and seas. There are four oceans, and smaller stretches of salt water—called seas—form part of them. The world's largest sea, the South China Sea, is part of the largest ocean, the Pacific. The waves, wind patterns, tides, and water currents of the four oceans all have a global effect, because the oceans are joined together. Life began in the oceans, and today their range of depths and temperatures provide different habitats for all kinds of plants and animals. The oceans form a major resource for humans, providing us with food, energy, and minerals.

OCEANS OF THE WORLD

There are four oceans, Atlantic, Pacific, Indian and Arctic. The world's largest ocean, the Pacific, is connected to the Atlantic and Indian Oceans in the southern waters around Antarctica. These waters are sometimes called the Southern, or Antarctic, Ocean. In the other polar region, the Arctic is connected to the Pacific and Atlantic Oceans by straits and seas.

OCEAN SIZE

Pacific Ocean:
181,300,000 sq km (70,000,000 sq mi)

Atlantic Ocean:
82,399,918 sq km (31,814,640 sq mi)

Arctic Ocean:
14,055,930 sq km (5,427,000 sq mi)

Indian Ocean:
73,427,795 sq km (28,350,500 sq mi)

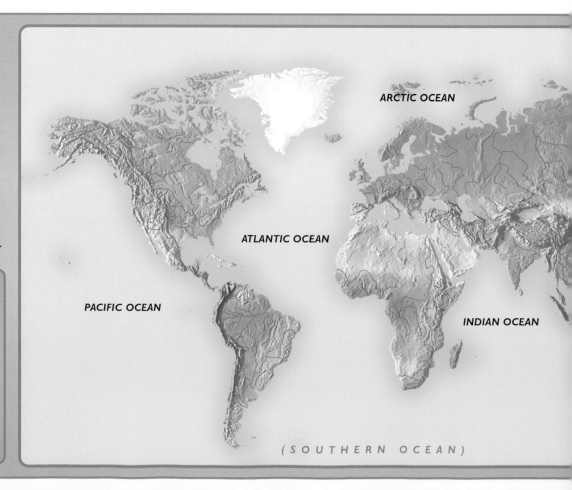

ARCTIC OCEAN

ATLANTIC OCEAN

PACIFIC OCEAN

INDIAN OCEAN

(S O U T H E R N   O C E A N)

OCEAN CURRENTS

The oceans are never still. As well as rising and falling tides, there are currents, which are like rivers in the sea. Near the ocean's surface, currents are swept along by the wind. Close to the Equator, winds blow mainly from east to west. Towards the poles, however, the direction is reversed, and ocean currents are mainly blown eastward. Deep-water currents are set in motion by differences in temperature and salt content of the water. The oceans are warmer near the Equator, where the Sun's heat is strongest. Nearer the poles, cold water sinks to the bottom and moves slowly toward the Equator. Generally, warm water rises through colder water.

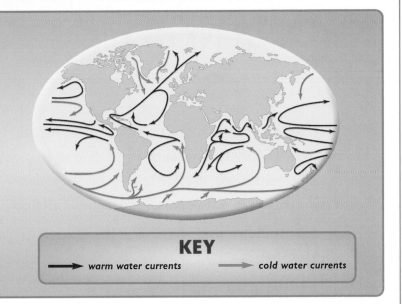

KEY

→ warm water currents   → cold water currents

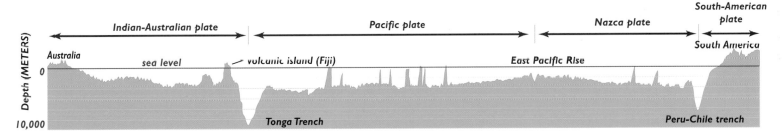

▲ ACROSS THE PACIFIC

If you took away all the water from the Pacific Ocean and stood on the ocean floor, this is what the land underneath would look like. The land covers more than 12,000 kilometers (7,450 miles), from Australia to South America. If you could make the journey along the ocean floor, you would start by moving down the gentle slope of the Australian continental shelf (see page 71). On your way you would come across many high mountains and deep valleys. The highest mountains reach above the surface of the ocean—the island of Fiji is actually the peak of a very high **volcano**. The deepest valley is the Tonga Trench, where the Pacific **plate** is forced beneath the Indian-Australian plate (see pages 16–19). The East Pacific Rise is a **spreading ridge** where new **crust** is formed, pushing the Pacific and Nazca plates apart.

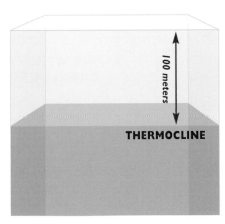

◄ WATER TEMPERATURE

The temperature of the ocean's surface at the North and South Poles is about -2 °C (28 °F). In winter, the water is cold enough to freeze into sheets of ice. Near the equator, the temperature of the surface water is about 30 °C (86 °F). Warmth goes down to a depth of about 100 meters (330 feet) deep. Then there is a sudden change in the temperature of the water. The next layer down is called the thermocline, and here the temperature drops rapidly. Above the thermocline the water is moved by wind, tides, and currents. Below the thermocline, there is no mixing of warm and cold water. The water stays cold.

SEE ALSO	
Moving Continents	**pages 16–17**
Ocean Floor	**pages 70–71**

OCEAN FLOOR

Beneath the waters of the oceans lies one of the most amazing places on Earth—the ocean floor. This part of Earth's surface has a varied landscape. Near land, there is a gently sloping area that forms a continental shelf. Moving farther away from land, the sea floor plunges down a steeper continental slope. When it flattens out, parts of the ocean floor forms large smooth regions known as **abyssal plains**, which are 4,000 to 6,000 meters (13,100 to 19,700 feet) below the surface of the sea. But just as on land, there are many other features to break up the flat plains. There are high mountain ranges and deep **canyons**. The highest mountains break through the surface of the ocean and form islands. Others, called **seamounts**, are tall mountains that are totally submerged. The ocean trenches, where one plate is forced beneath another, form the deepest valleys on Earth.

Trench

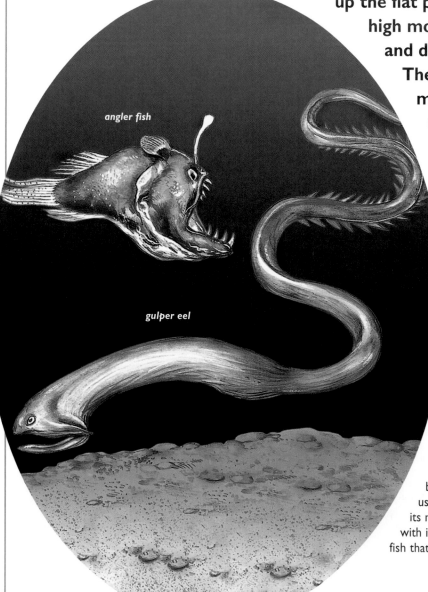
angler fish

gulper eel

◀ WEIRD DEEP OCEAN CREATURES

Underwater creatures have evolved some amazing features to survive at depths of more than 2,500 meters (8,000 feet). Light cannot penetrate further than 900 meters (2,900 feet) through the water, so beneath this the ocean is pitch black. The angler fish uses a light on its head to lure smaller creatures into its mouth. A gulper eel swims in the murky blackness with its huge mouth open wide ready to gulp down any fish that swims in its path.

UNDERWATER LANDSCAPE

The underwater landscape has mountains, valleys, and plains. The plains are called **abyssal plains** and the valleys are called trenches. The mountains are called **seamounts**, which are volcanic in origin, and are are mostly cone-shaped. The tallest single seamount reaches up 4,000 meters (13,100 feet) from the ocean floor without breaking the surface of the water. Flat-topped underwater mountains are called **guyots**. Some mountains break through the surface as islands. The Hawaiian volcano of Mauna Kea rises 10,203 meters (33,476 feet) above the floor of the Pacific Ocean, and more than half this height is below the surface of the ocean. This is the world's tallest mountain from base to peak. The world's deepest valley is also underwater. The Mariana Trench, in the Pacific Ocean, dives to 11,022 meters (36,160 feet) below sea level.

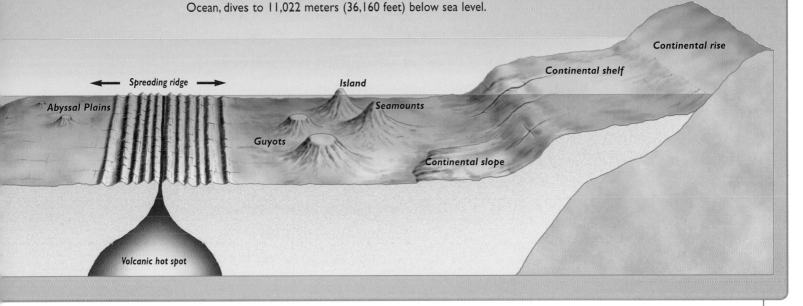

Spreading ridge

Island

Seamounts

Continental rise

Continental shelf

Abyssal Plains

Guyots

Continental slope

Volcanic hot spot

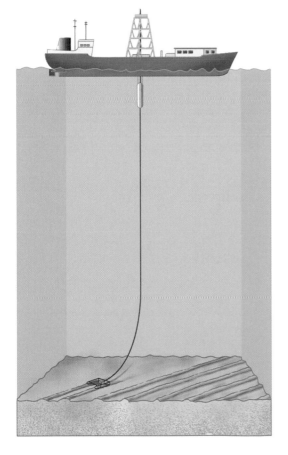

EXPLORATION ▶

Scientists study the deep oceans using submarines or submersibles, which are a smaller type of submarine. The seafloor can be mapped using echo sounding equipment. This sends out a series of signals through underwater loudspeakers. At other times explosions are set off near the submarine. The sound travels through the water to the seafloor and is bounced back toward the surface. Here, the time it has taken for the sound to travel is noted. From this, the depth of the water can be calculated. As the submarine moves across the ocean, the data is used to build a map, called a hydrographic chart, of the ocean floor.

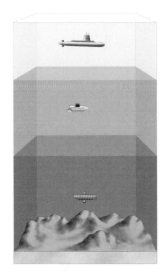

◀ DREDGING

Sand, gravel, and many valuable minerals can be scooped up from the sea floor by special ships called dredgers. In the Pacific, small black lumps called manganese nodules have been dredged from the ocean floor. The nodules contain iron, copper, and nickel, as well as manganese, and are valuable to industry.

SEE ALSO	
Moving Continents	**pages 16–17**
Oceans of the World	**pages 68–69**

ISLANDS

An island is a piece of land that is surrounded by water. Greenland is the largest island in the world. Australia and Antarctica are also surrounded by water, but they are such large land masses that we call them continents. Greenland is known as a continental island, because it once formed part of a larger land mass. Continental islands are cut off by erosion or by a rise in sea level. There are two other main kinds—volcanic and barrier islands. Volcanic islands, such as Japan and Iceland, formed when underwater volcanoes erupted and the resulting mountains reached above the sea. Barrier islands are formed when sand or sediment carried by rivers or sea currents pile up into banks. As sea levels rise around the world, some low-lying islands are lost.

◄ MANHATTAN, NEW YORK CITY

Manhattan is one of the busiest islands in the world. People working in Manhattan can get to work using bridges, tunnels, and ferries. Space was made for people to live and work on this crowded island by building upwards, creating some of the world's tallest skyscrapers. These were built on areas of strong bedrock which could support the tall buildings' deep foundations.

HOW A CORAL ATOLL IS FORMED

An atoll is a ring of coral, formed from the skeletons of billions of tiny marine animals. Coral islands surround a central circle of shallow water, called a lagoon. There are many atolls in the warm seas of the South Pacific Ocean.

A circular coral reef grows around the shoreline of a volcanic island. As the coral dies, it turns into rock.

When the volcano is no longer active and begins to sink, the coral forms a barrier reef around a lagoon of water.

The coral reef continues to grow as the volcano disappears beneath the surface, creating an atoll.

GREAT BARRIER REEF

The Great Barrier Reef, off the northeast coast of Australia, is an enormous chain of coral reefs. It stretches for more than 2,000 kilometers (1,240 miles), forming small coral islands where the reef breaks through the surface. Sand and soil build up on top of the coral islands, allowing plants to grow.

NEW VOLCANIC ▶ ISLAND

In November 1963, a volcano on the ocean floor off the coast of Iceland erupted. The eruption formed a new island, which was named Surtsey. The eruptions continued until 1967, by which time Surtsey had grown to 2.6 square kilometers (one square mile). Scientists were able to watch the island form, and see how quickly plants and animals appeared on it.

■ Reykjavik

ICELAND

Vestmannaeyjar

Surtsey

CONTINENTAL ISLAND

Mont-Saint-Michel, off the coast of Normandyin northwest France, is part of the continent of Europe. It is not yet a complete continental island. When the tide goes out, a thin strip of land known as a causeway connects the island of Mont-Saint-Michel to the mainland. When the tide comes in, the causeway is flooded and Mont-Saint-Michel becomes an island. If the sea level rises, Mont-Saint-Michel will become a permanent island.

SEE ALSO

Volcanoes	pages 26–27
Oceans of the World	pages 68–69

MAPPING THE WORLD

▲ OLD AND NEW WORLDS

As explorers discovered more of the world, they added their discoveries to existing maps and made new maps. The more information they had, the more accurate and useful the maps became. This map shows the view of the world in 1607, North America, South America, and Australia were not well charted.

Maps are used to show the position and shapes of countries, mountains, valleys, rivers, seas, and many other features. Maps are needed to navigate the seas, to travel abroad, and to understand our local area better. They help us to build a picture of the world as a whole—both its geological features and how it is broken up into countries—and see how the world is changing over time. Mapping a small area may be easy, but the world is round and maps are flat. Cartographers (mapmakers) have found ways of showing the world on paper. Using modern technology, including satellite photographs and computers, maps are now even more accurate.

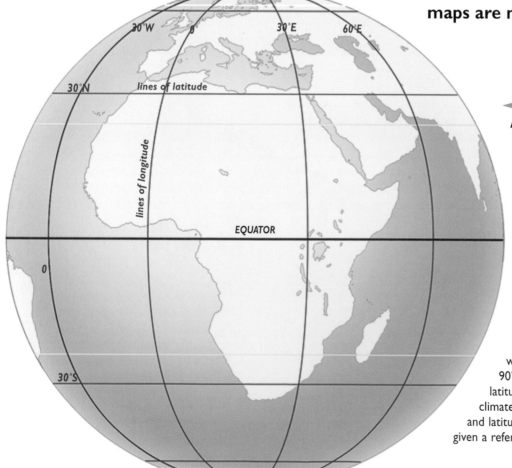

◀ LATITUDE AND LONGITUDE

Cartographers use a grid of imaginary lines drawn over the surface of Earth. All lines of longitude run through both the North and South Pole. These lines, called meridians, divide the world into 360°, with 0° running through Greenwich in England. They are used to mark out the world's time zones. Lines of latitude, called parallels, are drawn parallel to the Equator and are split up into 180°. The Equator is at 0° all the way around, while the two poles are 90° North and 90° South. Lines of latitude divide the Earth roughly into climate zones. Using degrees of longitude and latitude, any point on Earth can be given a reference position.

ONE WORLD, DIFFERENT VIEWS

Earth is a three-dimensional sphere. In order to show the whole surface of the sphere, it has to be cut and stretched on a flat, two-dimensional map. The different ways of stretching the surface are called projections. The Mercator projection, as shown left and below, is the most common view of the world.

POLITICAL MAPS

To show how the world is broken up into countries, cartographers use colors and labels. Each country's borders are charted and then the country is colored differently from its neighbor, so each country can be clearly seen.

PHYSICAL MAPS

To show the geological features of the world, cartographers add shading to show the height of the land—areas with no shading are flat lands and areas with much shading are mountainous. Cartographers also use color to show vegetation—the yellow areas are desert; the green areas are woodlands or farmland; the purple areas are mountains with no vegetation.

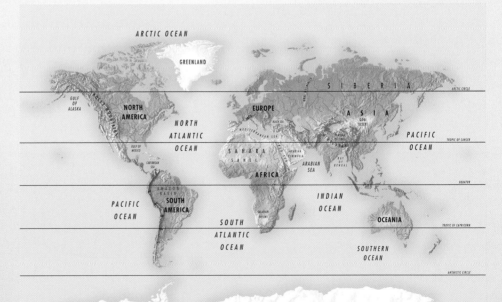

SEE ALSO	
Moving Continents	**pages 16–17**
Earth's Changing Surface	**pages 18–19**

MINING

TYPES OF MINES

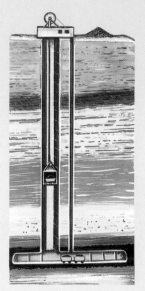

SHAFT MINE

DRIFT MINE

OPENCAST MINE

Once a mining company has found a possible site for a mine, it must apply for licenses and planning permission. This stage of working on a mine is known as evaluation, when local environmental concerns are taken into account. Geologists and engineers try to work out the economic and environmental costs of mining the area. They estimate the size of the deposit and recommend the best method of extracting it. Some minerals, such as coal, occur in thin layers, called seams. Seams may be reached from the surface by digging into a hillside and making a drift mine. Minerals that are just below the surface, such as copper and sometimes coal, may be dug out using an opencast (open-pit) mine. Shaft mines are used to reach minerals deep underground. Workers are lowered to the horizontal tunnels in an elevator called a cage.

Houses, roads, bridges, automobiles, and all the other products of our modern industrial society need a huge supply of **metals** and **minerals**. Most of our food and clothing come from things that grow on Earth's surface, but other raw materials have to be found underground and mined. The materials that we dig out of the ground are also used to make fuels, chemicals, and plastics. As the world's population increases, we need more and more mined materials, and industrial companies are constantly searching for new sources. The search has increased since it was realized that some materials, such as oil, may be in danger of running out during the course of the twenty-first century. As well as bringing wealth to a region, mining may also have a great effect on its landscape. Large mines cannot always be filled in when they have finished their useful production, and they often leave unsightly hills of debris. Responsible governments have found ways to landscape former mines, using hills and lakes formed during mining as recreational areas for local residents and wildlife.

◄ OPENCAST MINING

Surface mining is generally much less expensive than underground mining. This large coal mine *(left)* is in Alberta, Canada. Similar mines are also used to blast and dig out **ores**—rocks or minerals that contain a useful metal. In these mines, workers must first remove the overburden, which is the layer of **soil** and rock covering the ore deposits. Then they use explosives to break up the rocks containing the ore. They create a series of horizontal layers, called benches, each about 20 meters (66 feet) wide. Then they build roads to link up the benches at the side of the pit, so that trucks can be loaded to take the coal or ore to a processing plant *(see page 82)*.

▲ RESTORING THE ENVIRONMENT

Waste material from mining may be pumped into a so-called tailing pond (as shown above in the UK). The waste particles gradually settle to the bottom. Later, the area may be landscaped for use as a recreational area. Smaller mines and open pits may be landscaped. Gravel pits are sometimes turned into recreational areas with walks, picnic areas, and watersports.

◄ GRAVEL WORKS

Surface working and dredging of pits and ponds are used to mine gravel—loose deposits of small stones and rock fragments. Gravel is roughly the same size as pebbles on a beach—between 2 and 64 millimeters (0.08 and 2.5 inches). After being scooped up, the gravel is run along conveyor belts to be washed, sorted, and loaded onto trucks. Gravel is used in the making of concrete and to build roads.

HOW COAL FORMED

The plant layers soaked up water and were pressed together, forming a brown, spongy material called peat.

*More **sediment** layers formed on top of the peat, burying it deeper and deeper. The greater pressure and heat turned the peat into a brown coal called lignite.*

More heat and pressure, at greater depths, turned the lignite into a soft, black coal called bituminous coal.

This turned finally into a harder, shiny black coal called anthracite.

FOSSIL FUELS: COAL

Most of the energy that we use to power our factories, drive our vehicles, and heat our homes comes from substances that occur naturally in Earth's **crust**. We call these substances **fossil fuels**, and they occur in three different forms—as a solid (coal), a liquid (oil), and a gas (natural gas). They are called fossil fuels because they all formed from the fossilized remains of plants and animals which lived many millions of years ago. Most of the coal that we still mine today was made by trees and plants which lived in the **Carboniferous** period, 362 to 290 million years ago.

They were gradually buried and over millions of years pressure turned them into peat and then coal. Like all fossil fuels, coal is a non-renewable form of energy. It can only be used once, and we are not sure when supplies under the ground will be exhausted.

◀ CARBONIFEROUS SWAMPS

The photograph *(left)* shows fossils of a plant that lived in a swamp forest during the Carboniferous period. The name itself comes from the word carbon, which is a Latin term for "charcoal" and the name of the element that is present in coal. Most coal comes from the fern-like plants that lived in these swamps during the Mississippian and Pennsylvanian periods, which together make up the Carboniferous period *(see page 15)*. At that time the climate in the land masses that later became North America, Europe, and Asia was hot and wet. Some early giant trees grew as high as 30 meters (98 feet). Much smaller descendants of some of the trees and plants can still be found today.

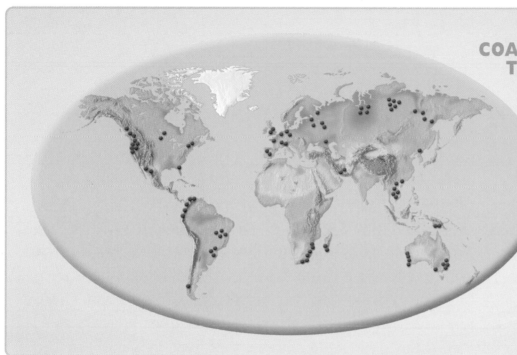

COAL AROUND THE WORLD

There are coal deposits on every continent, including Antarctica. There is also coal under the oceans, but it is mostly too difficult and expensive to mine. The world's largest producers of coal are China, United States, Russia, India, and Germany.

● *coal deposits*

◀ MECHANIZED MINING

As shown in this Russian mine, coal mining is now a highly mechanized process. Large machines move back and forth along the coal face, cutting away tons of coal at a time and passing it directly onto conveyor belts to be transported out of the mine. As the rock cutting machines move forward, they add roof supports to the tunnel behind. Men are still needed in the mines to look after the machines

◀ POLLUTION PROBLEMS

When fossil fuels are burned, they give off gases which pollute the atmosphere. At the same time these so-called greenhouse gases, which include carbon dioxide, trap solar heat near Earth. Scientists believe that in this way fossil fuels contribute to global warming, which in turn is causing the polar **ice caps** to melt and sea levels to rise.

FOSSIL FUELS: OIL AND GAS

TRAPPED UNDERGROUND

The oil and gas that formed millions of years ago was able to move within permeable, or porous, rocks. When it met impermeable, or non-porous, rocks, however, it became trapped and formed reservoirs. Geologists look for these reservoirs in order to locate the oil and gas, which are often found together.

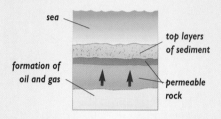

Oil and gas are able to move upwards through layers of permeable **sedimentary rocks**.

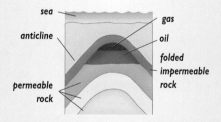

The oil and gas have become trapped beneath arch-shaped impermeable rock, forming a reservoir.

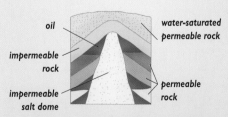

A huge dome of rock salt has been forced up by pressure, and this has trapped oil (colored gray) because it cannot pass through the salt.

Oil, or petroleum, and natural gas are both important fossil fuels. Crude oil, the form of petroleum that is found in its original state underground, is a thick, sticky, greenish liquid. Oil can also be extracted from solid rocks such as oil shale and tar sand. Natural gas is made up mainly of methane. Like petroleum, methane is a hydrocarbon—a mixture of hydrogen and carbon. These hydrocarbons were formed many millions of years ago from tiny plants and animals that lived in warm seas. When they died, their remains were covered on the sea floor by mud and sand. Over millions of years heat and pressure turned the organic remains into oil and gas, which was held between the solid rocks that formed out of the sediment. Many regions that were covered by oceans millions of years ago are now desert, though some large fuel deposits are still found beneath the ocean floor.

DRILLING FOR BLACK GOLD ▶

Oil is so valuable in our modern industrialized society that it has been called "black gold". In many of the world's oceans and seas, oil rigs are used to drill for both oil and gas. A fixed platform has drilling machinery and living quarters for workers. The platform rests on the sea floor on a framework of steel supports. The oil and gas are carried along pipelines to tankers or to a refinery on shore. There the crude oil is separated into different components to make gasoline, diesel oil, kerosene, and other forms of petroleum.

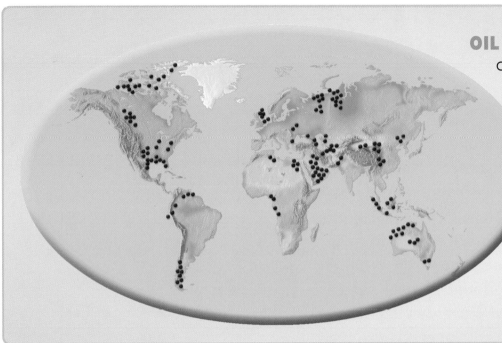

OIL RESERVES

Oil reserves have been found in many parts of the world. The world's largest producers of crude oil are Saudi Arabia, United States, Russia, Iran, and China. The discovery of oil beneath the Arabian Desert brought great wealth to Saudi Arabia and neighboring countries. The world's top producers of natural gas are Russia, United States, Canada, Netherlands, and the U.K.

● *oil reserves*

◀ DELIVERING GAS

When natural gas has been discovered by drilling, it is delivered to processing plants through pipelines. There the raw gas is cleaned, to rid it of sulfur, water, dust, and any other impurities. Before it is delivered to people's homes, a chemical odor is added to the gas. This is done because natural gas has no smell and any leaks might otherwise not be noticed.

FINDING FOSSIL FUELS

In order to locate **fossil fuels** beneath the ground, geologists collect data so that they can produce a cross-section map of rock layers. They do this by using explosives to create small artificial earthquakes. On land, they may also use a thumper truck to hit the ground and cause shock waves. The waves are reflected off the various rock layers beneath the ground, and returning signals are collected. At sea, explosive charges are set off beneath the surface. The returning signals are sensed by hydrophones. Geologists use computers to produce cross-sections, which tell them where fossil fuels are likely to be located and where they can be mined.

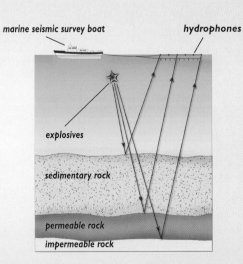

marine seismic survey boat

hydrophones

explosives

sedimentary rock

permeable rock

impermeable rock

SEE ALSO	
Mining	**pages 76–77**
Coal	**pages 78–79**

METALS

ALUMINUM

Aluminum is a silvery-white metal that was first discovered in 1827. There is more aluminum in Earth's **crust** than any other kind of metal. The main ore of aluminum is a rock called bauxite. Aluminum is lightweight and does not rust. It has many uses, from foil and cans in the kitchen to power lines across the country. Pure aluminum is soft, so the metal is often mixed with other metals, such as copper, to form hard alloys.

A **metal** is a chemical element, which means that it cannot be broken down into other substances. Metals are found underground in the rocks or minerals that we call **ores**. Ores are usually mined, though sometimes metals are found in river sands and gravels, in deposits called placers. There are about 70 metals, and although they vary in some of their qualities, such as hardness and strength, they have certain features in common. All metals are solid at room temperature (except mercury, which is liquid). They conduct heat and electricity well. Most metals are grayish in color. When they are polished, metals reflect light with a shine that is called metallic luster. We call especially beautiful and rare metals precious, while base metals are more common and considered to be useful rather than ornamental. Metals are particularly useful to us because they can be easily worked and shaped when they are hot.

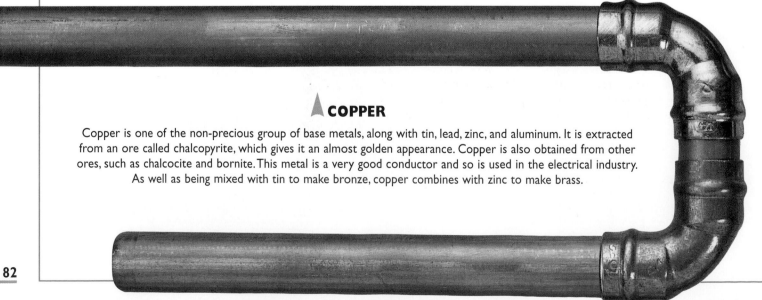

COPPER

Copper is one of the non-precious group of base metals, along with tin, lead, zinc, and aluminum. It is extracted from an ore called chalcopyrite, which gives it an almost golden appearance. Copper is also obtained from other ores, such as chalcocite and bornite. This metal is a very good conductor and so is used in the electrical industry. As well as being mixed with tin to make bronze, copper combines with zinc to make brass.

ALLOYS ▶

Mixtures of metals are called alloys. To make an alloy, metals are heated, then mixed and cooled until they are solid. Most alloys, like steel and brass, are harder than the metals from which they were made. Bronze *(right)* is a mixture of copper and tin. These metals soften at a low temperature and can be melted over a wood fire. Bronze was first used more than five thousand years ago. Today lead, nickel, and other metals are also added to the mixture to make special bronzes. Bronze alloy is used in the electrical industry. It is also used to make springs, machine bearings, bells, and statues.

◀ PRECIOUS METALS

Gold, silver, and platinum make up the group that we call precious metals. Gold is found in its pure form in between rock layers, or in river sands and gravel as dust or chunks called nuggets. It can also be found combined with the metal tellurium. It is scarce and valuable. Gold is easy to beat into thin sheets, called gold leaf, or draw out into wire. Gold conducts electricity well, and it does not react to most chemicals. It is used in scientific and electrical equipment. Gold is also used to make coins and jewelry, and to decorate books and buildings. South Africa mines more gold than any other country. Silver, which comes from argentite and lead ores, has been used for thousands of years to make coins and jewelry. Platinum was first discovered by an Italian scientist in 1557, and is now the most valuable precious metal.

ORES

Hematite *(right)* is the most important iron ore. It is commonly known as kidney ore, because of its bulbous shape. In its purest form, hematite consists of about 70 percent iron. Iron is also obtained from the ores limonite and magnetite. China is the world's biggest producer of iron ore. Other important ores are galena, from which lead is extracted, and cinnabar, which produces mercury. After an ore has been mined, it has to be processed at a special plant to extract the metal. First the ore is crushed into fine particles. These are then mixed with water, forming a muddy slurry. This is filtered and dried, leaving a mixture known as a concentrate. Heat and chemical processes are used to separate the metal from this concentrate.

SEE ALSO	
Rocks	**pages 36–37**
Minerals	**pages 42–43**
Mining	**pages 76–77**

STONES FOR BUILDING AND DECORATING

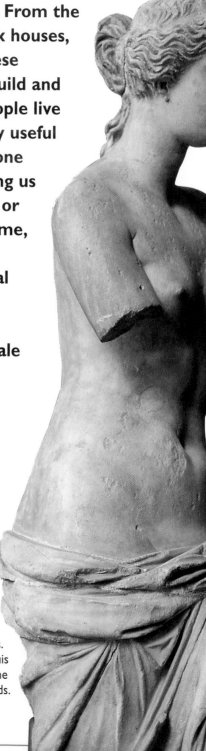

People have been using rocks and stones for many thousands of years. From the earliest caves to mud huts, brick houses, stone temples, and palaces, these materials have been used to build and decorate the places where people live and work. They are particularly useful materials, because rock and stone are strong and durable, providing us with protection from wet, cold, or stormy weather. At the same time, they form cool buildings in hot climates. We still dig a great deal of rock and stone out of the ground, using both traditional methods of mining and large-scale quarrying techniques. Just as in the past, stone is still used by architects for buildings, and by artists for sculpture and many forms of ornamentation.

Modern builders also use concrete, which is a mixture of water with limestone, clay, sand, and gravel.

▲ CLAY BRICKS

Clay is formed into a regular shape and fired (heated) in a kiln (oven) to a temperature of about 1,000 °C (1,830 °F). Clay has been used to make bricks for thousands of years. Adobe bricks, made of mud and straw and dried in the sun, were used in Mesopotamia (part of modern Iraq) 8,000 years ago. In warm climates, such as Mexico, adobe houses are still made.

VENUS DE MILO ▶

White marble has always been a favorite material with sculptors. In 1820, a farmer plowing his field on the Greek island of Milos was surprised when he dug up a statue of Aphrodite, the goddess of love and beauty. The sculpture was later found to have been made around 200 B.C., from marble quarried on the nearby island of Paros. A French naval officer bought Aphrodite (called Venus by the Romans) for King Louis XVIII. The famous Venus de Milo ("Venus from Milos") was then put on show in the Louvre museum, in Paris, France, where she still stands.

▲ MEGALITHS

Megaliths are large stones used as monuments. They have been put up for thousands of years by different cultures all over the world. The ancient stones of Stonehenge *(above)*, on Salisbury Plain in England, are more than 3,500 years old. Builders may have used wooden rollers and ropes to put them in place. No one knows why the stone circles were built, but they may have been used to follow the movements of the Sun and Moon.

TOMBS AND MONUMENTS

Stone makes a long-lasting monument to human achievements. But acid rain and pollution affects buildings and sculptures, eroding intricate carvings and wearing away the stone. The face of the Great Sphinx at Giza, near Cairo, Egypt, has been damaged by wind and rain. It was built with the Great Pyramids as tombs by the ancient Egyptians around 2,600 B.C. Inside the pyramids are hidden a complex array of tunnels and burial chambers. Building them was a feat in itself. The pyramids and the Sphinx are made of nummulitic limestone. This is named after the many fossils of marine nummulites that formed in the stone. The Great Pyramid is made from more than two million limestone blocks.

FLINT ▶

This ancient arrowhead is made of flint, which was widely used in prehistoric times. A form of the mineral silica, this sedimentary rock can be chipped to give a sharp cutting edge. When it breaks, flint leaves a conchoidal fracture *(see page 42)*. It was also used to make sparks and create fire, and is still used in buildings today.

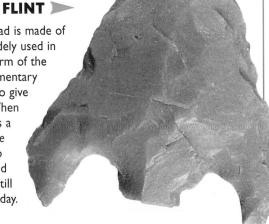

SEE ALSO	
Rocks	**pages 36–37**
Mining	**pages 76–77**

GEMSTONES

Gemstones are **minerals** that are considered beautiful and precious enough to be used in jewelry or as ornaments. Of the thousands of different minerals, about fifty are used as gemstones, including diamonds, rubies, and emeralds. Gemstones need to be hard to withstand use, and many of the non-precious minerals are too soft or brittle. When they are mined, most gemstones have an irregular shape and a rough texture, so they are cut and polished to make them more beautiful to the human eye.

◀ RUBIES

These uncut rubies show typical triangular surface markings. Ruby is the best known red-colored gemstone. It is a form of the mineral corundum, whose chemical name is aluminum oxide. Corundum can contain very small amounts of chemical elements, called trace elements, which create the color. Ruby contains the trace elements chromium and vanadium. These stones will look even more beautiful when they have been cut and polished.

CUTTING A DIAMOND

An octahedral (eight-faced) diamond is cut in several stages.

| 1 | 2 | 3 | 4 | 5 | 6 |

The process begins with an eight-sided diamond

The top of the crystal is sawn off and put aside, to cut as another, smaller gem.

The edge of the larger part is rounded.

The flat polished surfaces, called facets, are then ground and polished.

The number of facets and their angles are chosen to give the best sparkle.

◄ BRILLIANT DIAMOND

Experts who cut and polish gemstones to bring out their beauty are called lapidaries. In a well-cut gemstone, light entering the stone from the front is reflected off the surface of the stone and back through it to the front, so that it sparkles. The diamond set in this ring has a round shape with 58 facets, which is called a "brilliant cut."

IMITATION GEMSTONE

Imitation gemstones are made to look like the natural stone, but they have a different chemistry. They can be made of anything, including other minerals. Often, glass or plastic is used. This imitation opal (left) shows the flashes of color called the "play of color," similar to that of a natural opal.

SAPPHIRES ►

Like red ruby, blue sapphire is a form of corundum. Trace elements of iron and titanium give the blue color, which varies from one region to another. The Kashmir blue sapphire is the most highly prized color. The color of a sapphire can be improved by methods such as heat treatment.

synthetic emeralds

◄ GROWING YOUR OWN ►

Synthetic gemstones are made by scientists in laboratories. They can be made in hours or days, rather than in the millions of years that it takes for natural gemstones to form in rocks. Synthetic gemstones have the same chemistry as the natural gemstone. This means that the optical and physical properties (how they look and feel) are more or less the same as natural stones. Synthetic rubies and sapphires have been made in the laboratory for nearly a hundred years. They are made by melting aluminum oxide over burning oxygen and hydrogen.

cut emeralds

natural emeralds in rock

SEE ALSO	
Minerals	**pages 42–43**
Crystals	**pages 44–45**

ORGANIC GEMS

Some organic materials, which come originally from animals or plants, are also used as gems. Organic gems are often carved and fashioned as beads. The substances with an animal origin include many types of shells, as well as the pearls which sometimes form inside them. Different forms of coral are also used for necklaces and bracelets. The two best known plant-based gems are amber and jet. Yellow amber comes from prehistoric trees, and black jet is a special variety of lignite coal. All of these organic substances have been used since humans began making jewelry and ornaments.

◀ SHELL

Shells form the hard outer coverings of many mollusks. They are used as buttons, beads, knife handles, and for inlay work on decorated items, such as boxes.

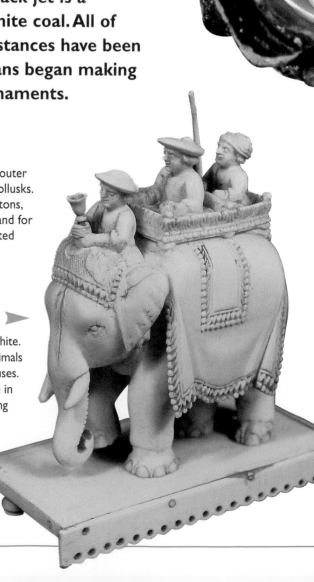

IVORY ▶

Ivory is hard and creamy-white. It comes from the tusks of animals such as elephants and walruses. Many countries do not allow trade in ivory. This is to protect elephants from being killed for their tusks. Fossil ivory or bone from dinosaurs, mammoths, and mastodons can also be dyed, carved, and fashioned as jewelry and other decorative items. Governments and organizations that protect animals encourage the use of alternatives, such as plastic, horn, and vegetable ivory made from nuts. This reduces the demand for real ivory.

◀ PEARL

Pearls are formed in seashells, particularly mollusks, such as oysters and mussels. Each seashell species forms different and distinctive pearls. Natural pearls form inside the shell when a piece of grit gets inside and acts as an irritant. The mollusk lays down layers of nacre (mother-of-pearl) around the grit. These layers build up to form a pearl. Pearls can also be cultured, or made by putting grit into a mollusk's shell deliberately. This is done on large pearl farms, set up in fresh or salt water.

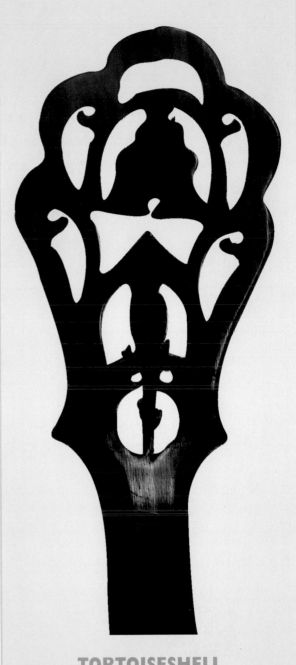

AMBER ▶

Amber is the fossilized resin of pine trees. The most famous sources are the countries around the Baltic Sea, such as Poland, Sweden, and Denmark. Amber also comes from Burma (Myanmar), Sicily, and the Dominican Republic. Amber can be heated to remove bubbles and make the amber clear.

TORTOISESHELL

Hair combs, boxes, and buttons all used to be made of tortoiseshell. This is the shell of the hawksbill turtle. Tortoiseshell has a distinctive pattern. Today, plastic imitations replace real tortoiseshell. So many hawksbill turtles have been hunted that they are now an endangered species.

SEE ALSO

Crystals	pages 44–45
Gemstones	pages 86–87

GLOSSARY

abyssal plain - *flat plains of the ocean floor*

asteroid - *a large piece of rock in space, left over from when the planets formed*

asthenosphere - *partially molten layer in the mantle upon which the plates of the lithosphere move*

atmosphere - *the air that surrounds Earth. It can be divided into four layers: troposphere, stratosphere, mesosphere, and the outermost layer, the thermosphere. Beyond the thermosphere is the exosphere and outer space.*

atoll - *a circle of coral islands surrounding a central lagoon that was formed around a volcanic island that is now submerged*

basin - *a hollow in Earth's surface where a lake forms*

beach - *the area between the cliff line and the lowest tides, usually made up of rock, pebbles, or sand*

Big Bang - *what scientists call the explosion that blew the Universe into existence*

biosphere - *area where life is found on Earth*

canyon - *a deep valley with almost vertical sides, gouged out by a river*

cave - *a natural hollow space formed mainly in rock*

cirque - *the area where ice collects and a glacier starts*

cleavage - *a preferred plane along which a mineral may break, related to planes of weakness in the atomic structure of the mineral*

cliff - *the rock face exposed to the sea*

clint - *pavement of limestone blocks separated by cracks and joints called grikes, formed by the dissolution of limestone*

conglomerate - *a coarse-grained sedimentary rock. Rounded fragments are held together by a mineral cement*

convection - *the process where hot substances rise and cool substances sink*

continental drift - *theory suggesting that Earth's continents have moved position (drifted) relative to one another*

core - *the center of Earth, made up of two layers: a solid inner core and a liquid outer core*

crater - *the round sunken area at the top of a volcano or the round hole made by a meteorite impact*

crust - *the outermost layer of Earth, made of continental crust and oceanic crust*

crystal - *a mineral with a regular, geometric shape, usually with a smooth face and straight edges*

desert - *a region that has less than ten centimeters (four inches) of rain a year*

earthquake - *a sudden, violent movement in Earth's crust*

epicenter - *the point on Earth's surface immediately above the focus of an earthquake*

erosion - *the process of wearing away rocks and landscapes by weathering*

estuary - *where freshwater mixes with seawater at the mouth of a river*

evolution - *the slow adaptation of lifeforms to changes in environment*

extrusive igneous rock - *igneous rock that has formed from lava erupted from volcanoes*

fault - *where a crack occurs in rock or earth's crust*

firn - *old, dense, granular compacted snow, representing a stage in the alteration of fresh snow to glacier ice*

focus - *the place within Earth where an earthquake starts because of movement of rock*

fjord - *a former glacial valley with steep sides and a U-shaped profile, now containing seawater*

floodplain - *an area of land which is flooded when a river bursts its banks*

fossil - *remains or traces of animals and plants preserved in rock*

fossil fuel - *heat-producing matter that is formed by the fossilized remains of plants and animals*

fracture - *a break in a rock or mineral that is not related to its atomic structure*

gemstone - *a decorative material, usually a mineral, attributed with some or all of the qualities of rarity, beauty, and durability*

geology - *the science that studies Earth, its shape and what it is made of, how it changes and what causes the changes over time*

geyser - *hot fountain of water or steam from underground waters heated by volcanic activity*

glacier - *large mass of ice that persists throughout the year and flows downhill under its own weight*

grike - *cracks and joints that separate the blocks of rock called clints, of a pavement of limestone, formed by the dissolution of limestone*

guyot - *flat-topped submarine (undersea) mountain*

hot spot - *a very hot area of Earth's mantle, which causes volcanic eruptions in the middle of a plate*

humus - *the organic matter in soil which is produced by the breakdown and decomposition of plants and animals*

ice age - *a period of intense cold where much of Earth is covered by ice*

ice cap - *a large area of thick ice covering the Antarctic continent and the Arctic Ocean*

igneous rock - *rock formed from the solidification of magma or lava*

intrusive igneous rock - *igneous rock that solidifies beneath Earth's surface.*

karst - *landscape made of limestone*

landslide - *a mass movement downhill of rock and soil*

lava - *magma that reaches Earth's surface, erupted from volcanoes*

lithification - *the process of changing sediments to solid rock, usually by squashing (compressing) or sticking together (cementation)*

lithosphere - *the outer layer of Earth situated above the asthenosphere and which contains the crust and upper part of the mantle*

luster - *describes the surface and appearance of minerals and crystals*

magma - *molten rock material beneath Earth's surface (see lava)*

mantle - *Earth's main layer, between the core and the crust*

matrix - *fine-grained material that acts as a cement to form sedimentary rock*

meander - *a loop-like bend in a river or stream*

metal - *a chemical element that is usually solid at room temperature, conducts heat and electricity and has a shiny appearance*

metamorphic rock - *rock whose original mineralogy, texture or composition has* been changed by the effects of heat and/or pressure

meteorites - *rocks from outer space that land on the surface of Earth*

mid-ocean ridge - *see spreading ridge*

mineral - *naturally occuring inorganic substance with a constant chemical compostion and crystalline structure*

Mohs' Scale of Hardness - *a table showing the hardness of minerals*

moraine - *the rock fragments that are carried down a mountain by a glacier*

ore - *a mineral that contains large quantities of metal*

ozone layer - *layer in the upper atmosphere where the gas ozone is concentrated. It shields us from harmful ultra violet (UV) radiation from the Sun*

paleontologist - *a scientist who studies fossils, their lives and evolution*

plates - *the different sections of Earth's crust, of which some are continental plates and others are oceanic plates (otherwise* known as tectonic plates)

plate margin - *where two plates meet (otherwise known as plate boundary)*

plate tectonics - *a model which unifies the theories of continental drift and sea-floor spreading, and gives an explanation for earthquake and volcanic activity based upon the relative motion of Earth's plates*

prevailing wind - *the usual or common wind direction that persists for some time in an area*

pyroclastic flow - *pyroclastic material that flows down the side of a volcano during an eruption*

rainshadow desert - *an inland desert behind coastal mountains*

regolith - *the layer of rock and rock fragments that covers most of Earth's land surface*

Richter scale - *a measure of earthquake intensity (0–10) based on the size and speed of shock waves travelling through the ground*

rift valley - *sinking of a*

narrow strip of crust between parallel faults

Ring of Fire - *a belt of volcanoes around the edge of the Pacific Ocean*

rock - *a solid made of one or more minerals*

scree - *mass of boulders and rock fragments at the bottom of cliffs and mountain slopes, which have fallen from the rocks above*

seamount - *an isolated volcano that rises high above the sea floor*

sediment - *tiny particles of rock that are carried and deposited by water*

sedimentary rock - *rock formed by mineral grains or rock fragments that have been transported and deposited as sediment, and then pressed or stuck together*

seismic wave - *shock wave from an earthquake*

seismologist - *a scientist who studies earthquakes, seismic waves and their propagation through Earth*

sinkhole - *a dip in the*

ground where soluable rock has been dissolved and removed by groundwater

soil - *the part of the regolith where plants can grow, made from rock fragments, minerals and organic matter, water, and air*

solar system - *the Sun and the planets that orbit it, also the asteroids, comets, meteors and moons that orbit the planets*

spreading ridge - *a long line of volcanic mountains down the middle of an ocean, which marks where tectonic plates are moving apart and new oceanic crust is being erupted (otherwise known as mid-ocean ridge)*

stack - *a tall pillar of rock that once formed part of a cliff but has been eroded by the sea*

stalactite - *an icicle-shaped mineral deposit hanging from the roof of a cave*

stalagmite - *an icicle-shaped mineral deposit that builds up from the cave floor, beneath a stalactite*

streak - *color of a mineral in its powdered form*

subduction - *the process of one plate being forced beneath another*

tectonic plates - *see plates*

trade winds - *winds that blow from high pressure regions of sub-tropical belts towards regions of low pressure at the Equator*

tremor - *a movement of Earth's surface due to earthquake activity*

tsunami - *destructive seismic sea waves caused by earthquakes, volcanic eruptions or landslides under the sea*

volcanic eruptions - *when magma explodes through Earth's crust*

volcano - *an opening in the crust through which magma is erupted as lava*

watercycle - *the cycle of water from when it leaves Earth's surface through evaporation to when it returns*

weathering - *physical and chemical processes that break down the rocks on Earth's surface*

INDEX